AZERBAIJANI-ENGLISH
ENGLISH-AZERBAIJANI

DICTIONARY AND PHRASEBOOK

NICHOLAS AWDE
and
FAMIL ISMAILOV

SHIRE

D0318496

L494.
361

© 1999 Nicholas Awde

Hippocrene Books, Inc.
171 Madison Avenue
New York, NY 10016

ISBN 0-7818-0684-4 (pbk.)

Typesetting by Nicholas Awde/Desert♥Hearts

Printed in the United States of America

CONTENTS

- An Azerbaijani person is an **Azärbayjanlı**.
- The adjective for Azerbaijani is **Azärbayjanı**.
- Azerbaijanis call themselves **Azärbayjanlılar**.
- The Azerbaijani language is **Azärbayjan dili**.
- Azerbaijan is **Azärbayjan**.

INTRODUCTION

zerbaijan is a relatively young nation, although the land itself is very ancient. The precise age of its capital, Baku (or **Bakı**), is still the subject of much debate. Archeological remains unearthed in Baku's Old City (**İcheri Sheher**) date as far back as the 5th century A.D., and the first written record of the city is from the pen of an Arab traveller who wrote in 930 A.D. Some historians believe that Baku was founded by the Persian Emperor Darius (6th century A.D.)

The name of Azerbaijan was first used for the country and its people in the 19th century and eventually given its official seal by Muhammed Emin Rasulzade, the leader of the first Azerbaijani Democratic Republic in 1920. Up to this point, in the official documents and literature of the Russian Empire, Azerbaijanis were called 'Caucasian Tatars' (as opposed to the Crimean or Kazan Tatars) or, simply, 'Turks.'

Today, the vast majority of Azerbaijanis are spread across the republic of Azerbaijan, which has a total population of more than 7.5 million inhabitants, and Iran, where Azerbaijanis make up almost 20 million — about one third of the country's citizens.

Azerbaijanis hold a deep-rooted sense of the heritage handed down to them from the greater family of Turkic nations. Throughout the first millennium, tribes of nomadic Oghuz Turks came from the east and intermarried with the local people, which resulted in the great mixture of Turkic culture, Zoroastrian and — later in history — Islamic values.

The name, however, of the country and its people comes from Arabic/Persian and means 'Land of Fire.'

This is a clear reference to Azerbaijan's principal and vast natural wealth — its oil.

Azerbaijanis have used oil for centuries to light and heat their homes, to insulate roofs and even as medicine. The Zoroastrians worshipped it as a source of the Eternal Flame, while Marco Polo wrote that "it is not used in cooking, but burned in lamps, and used as a cure for a number of ailments."

The first paraffin plant in the world was built in 1823 to process Baku oil. Later, the first commercial oil well was drilled in Azerbaijan in 1875, a fact which also marked the beginning of the oil boom and put Baku firmly on the world map. International oil giants like the Nobel Brothers, Standard Oil and other companies all came and made their fortunes in the Baku oil fields.

In the late 19th to early 20th century one third of the world's entire oil market came from Azerbaijan. The oil boom not only created local family fortunes for new Azerbaijani, Armenian and Russian millionaires but also established a link between Azerbaijani and European culture which has left Azerbaijan forever a crossroads between West and East, Christianity and Islam.

The Russian Empire made its first moves to take over Azerbaijan in the 19th century. Initially, the Tsars annexed a number of Azerbaijani principalities (including Baku) in 1806. Later, a series of agreements ended the Russo-Persian wars, and the Turkmenchay Pact between Russia and Persia drew up borders between the two states along the river Arax, dividing Azerbaijan into two parts: Northern and Southern Azerbaijan.

Northern Azerbaijan, which included Baku, Gyanja (or **Gänjä**) and other major cities, developed under the influence of Russian and European cultures, growing more open and tolerant towards mixed cosmopolitan society. Southern Azerbaijan, for its part, persisted more within a traditional communal culture under the rule of the Persian Shahs.

Azerbaijan's drive for independence in the 1920s was soon blocked by the Red Army, sent by Lenin to support local Bolsheviks in taking over the country and its much-needed oil. The Republic of Azerbaijan finally became a part of the Soviet Union in 1922.

Seventy years of Soviet rule have not left the Azerbaijani people without problems — not only the memory of Stalinist repressions, but more recent factors such as the brain-drain flowing ever outwards (for example, the oil reserves of Siberia were prospected and developed by Azerbaijani oilmen, while about a million Azeris still live in Russia's Tyumen oil region), or compulsory agricultural policies like growing of cotton.

The people of Azerbaijan finally achieved their independence in 1991 and, despite the war with Armenia over the Nagorno-Karabakh region, they now look forward to a future that looks set to put their nation firmly back on the world map. So wherever you go, you will always be met with the traditional cry of **"Khosh gälmishsiniz!"** — "Welcome!"

~

A VERY BASIC GRAMMAR

Azerbaijani belongs to the Altaic family of languages, Other members of this group include Uzbek and Kazakh, but Azerbaijani's closest neighbor, linguistically speaking, is Turkish — and speakers of the two are able to understand each other with little difficulty.

Until the beginning of the 20th century, Azerbaijani was written in an Arabic-based script, which is still continued south of the border in Iran. Over the following decades, in the republic of Azerbaijan, there were various moves to convert the language to Roman and then a modified Cyrillic alphabet. With independence, a new, Turkish-based Roman script has been successfully introduced (see page 18).

STRUCTURE OF THE LANGUAGE

While totally unrelated to English, the structure of Azerbaijani is nevertheless quite simple. In word order, the verb is usually put at the end of the sentence, e.g.

Män evä gediräm.
'I go home.' (literally: 'I home go.')

Azerbaijani is virtually free of grammatical irregularities, and this helped by the fact that it is an 'agglutinative' language, meaning that it adds information at the end of the word in clear, distinct segments, e.g.

dad 'taste'
dad-lı 'tasty'
dad-sız 'tasteless'

ish 'work'
ish-siz 'work-less' (= 'unemployed')
ish-siz-lik 'work-less-ness' (= 'unemployment')

Although a trifle extreme, you can build up clearly understandable words like **sämtläshdirilmishlärdän** — 'from one of those who has been orientated.' Basically this breaks down as **sämt** 'orientated' + **läsh** *verbal ending* + **dir** 'who' + **il** *passive* + **mish** *past* + **lär** *plural* + **dän** 'from'!

VOWEL & CONSONANT 'HARMONY'

Many words can change their vowels. This may look a little strange at first, but there are very regular rules underlying this — if you listen to the spoken language, you'll realize that this is what adds much of the distinctive 'color' that makes Turkic languages so distinctive in sound, since they all share this same feature. There are two linked groups of vowels:

front vowels: **ä, e, i, ö, ü**
back vowels: **a, ı, o, u**

Although words of foreign origin may be exceptions, each originally Azerbaijani word tends to have all of its vowels of the same type, i.e. all front or all back. This phenomenon is called vowel harmony. This is taken one step further with the many suffixes in the language which have 'floating vowels.' These change their vowel(s) to 'harmonise' with the preceding vowels of the word they are modifying. Some have only a two-way change, others a four-way change, e.g.

Two-way vowel harmony:
    -dän 'from' — *front* **evdän** 'from the houses'
                  back **daghdan** 'from the mountains'

Four-way vowel harmony:
    -siz 'without' — *front* **ishsiz** 'without work'
                         kürksüz 'without a coat'
                  back **dadsız** 'without taste
                         pulsuz 'without money'

There are some instances where this affects consonants as well. One common example where the vowel and the consonant changes is the infinitive ending **-mäk** or **-maq**, e.g.

front **istämäk** 'to want'
back **almaq** 'to take'

NOUNS

Azerbaijani has no words for 'the,' 'a' or 'an' in the same way as English does — instead the meaning is generally undestood from the context, e.g. **kishi** can mean 'the man,' 'a man' or just simply 'man.'

Nouns form their plural by simply adding **-lär/-lar**, e.g. **ofis** 'office' — **ofislär** 'offices,' **mashın** 'car' — **mashınlar** 'cars.'

The genitive form is **-(n)in** — which changes its vowel, e.g. **ofis-in** 'office's,' **kitab-ın** 'book's,' **üz-ün** 'face's,' **futbol-un** 'football's.' For more on genitive constructions, see the section on possessives.

Azerbaijani is a great language for active wordbuilding, and four important suffixes to note are: **-chi** 'one who does, -er,' e.g. **ish** 'work' — **ishchi** 'worker,' **yazı** 'writing' — **yazıchı** 'writer'; **-ja/-jä** creates a language, e.g. **Azärbaijan** 'Azerbaijan' — **Azärbaijanja** 'Azerbaijani (language),' **Yaponiya** 'Japan' — **Yaponja** 'Japanese (language)'; **-lik/-lıq** makes 'concept' nouns, e.g. **nazir** 'minister' — **nazirlik** 'ministry,' **azad** 'free' — **azadlıq** 'freedom.'

ADJECTIVES

Adjectives are like nouns in that they can take the same endings. They always come before the noun, e.g.

| 'new' **täzä** | — | **täzä mashın** 'new car' |
| 'old' **köhnä** | — | **köhnä mashın** 'old car' |

Some basic adjectives are:

open **achıq**	quick **tez**
shut **baghlı**	slow **yavash**
cheap **ujuz**	big **böyük**
expensive **baha**	small **balaja**
hot **isti**	old **goja**
cold **soyuq**	young **javan**
near **yakhın**	good **yakhshı**
far **uzaq**	bad **pis**

A common way of creating adjectives from other words is

to add **-li/lı/lü/lu** at the end of a word, e.g. **Azärbayjanlı** 'Azerbaijani', **dadlı** 'tasty', etc. Adding **-siz/sız/süz/suz** gives the meaning of 'without' or '-less', e.g. **dadsız** 'tasteless'.

ADVERBS
Most adverbs have a single form which never changes. Some examples:

here **burada**	up **yukharı**
there **orada**	down **ashaghı**
well **yakhshı**	now **indi**
badly **pis**	tomorrow **sabah**

Some add special endings, like **yavashja** 'slowly' (from **yavash** 'slow'), while others have the same form as the corresponding adjective, e.g. **chevik** means 'rapid' or 'rapidly'.

POSTPOSITIONS
Azerbaijani has postpositions — where words like 'in,' 'at' and 'behind' come <u>after</u> the noun and not before it as in English (though remember that you can say 'who *with*?' as well as 'with who?' — and there's no change in meaning). They sometimes modify the ending of the word and can be joined:

to **-a/-ä**	under **altında**
at; in **-da/-dä**	after **dalında**
from **-dan/-dän**	in front of **qabaghında**

e.g. **Azerbaijan-da** 'in Azerbaijan,' **İngiltärä-dän** 'from England.'

PRONOUNS
Personal pronouns can add on endings just like nouns. Basic forms are as follows:

SINGULAR	PLURAL
I **män**	we **biz**
you *singular* **sän**	you *plural* **siz**
he/she/it **o**	they **onlar**

Possessive pronouns:

SINGULAR	PLURAL
my **-(i)m**	our **-(i)miz**
your **-(i)n**	your **-(i)iniz**
his/her/its **-(s)i**	their **-(s)i**

e.g. **ofisim** 'my office'
ofisi 'his/her/its/their office'
ofisimiz 'our office'

These change their vowels according to the four-way system.*

Postpositions add onto these endings, e.g. **mäktäb-im-dän** 'from my school' (literally: 'school-my-from').

Possessive pronouns are also used to express a variety of possession and other relationships between words. This form gives us 'of,' e.g. e.g. **Ali televizori** (literally: 'Ali his television') = 'Ali's television' (or 'the television of Ali'). This also gives us constructions like: **khalq musiqisi** 'folk music,' **ofis ishchisi** 'office worker,' etc.

Use the dictionary section to work out what these genitive constructions meaning:

yol polisi	**rok konserti**
dagh yolu	**peyk telefonu**
futbol matchı	

Demonstratives:

bu this	**bunlar** these
o that	**onlar** those

VERBS

Verbs are very easy to form, and add a wide number of suffixes to the end of the basic verb form. While the structure of Azerbaijani verbs is very different from English, in fact it is extremely logical and clearly set out, although in practise it can sometimes be a little difficult to extract the necessary information packed in at the end of each verb.

* Other forms in full are: **-(i)m/(ü)m/(u)m, -(i)n/(ü)n/(u)n, -(s)ı/(s)ü/(s)u, -(i)mız/(ü)müz/(u)muz, -(i)nız/(ü)nüz/(u)nuz, -(s)ı/(s)ü/(s)u.**

It is worth spending a little time sorting out the concept, and then you will meet with little difficulty in working out the distinct parts of an Azerbaijani sentence!

Every Azerbaijani verb has a basic form that carries a basic meaning. To the end of this are added smaller words or single vowels that add further information to tell you who's doing what and how and when, e.g.

görmäk 'to see'
gördüm 'I saw'
görüräm 'I see'
göräräm 'I may see'
göräjäyäm 'I will see'

Other endings carry even more information, e.g.

gejikmäk 'to be late'
gejikdirmäk 'to make late'
gejiklashdirmäk 'to be running late'

We saw the personal pronouns above, but these are only used for emphasis. Like French or Spanish, the verb already gives this information:

SINGULAR	PLURAL
I **-m**	we **-ik**
you *singular* **-n**	you *plural* **-siniz**
he/she/it **-i(r)**	they **-lär**

e.g. **görim** I see **görik** we see
görin you see **görsiniz** you see
göri he/she/it sees **görlär** they see

You'll see that these are similar in form to the possessive pronouns, and they also follow a changing vowel system.*

Mi/mı is placed at the end of the sentence to reinforce when a question is being asked, e.g. **Avtobus varmı?** 'Is there a bus?', or with longer sentences such as **Siz İngilishjä danıshırsınızmı?** 'Do you speak English?'

* Other forms in full are: -ı(r)/ü(r)/u(r), -ıq, -sınız/sünüz/sunuz, -lar.

Negatives vary in form according to tense. **Ma** 'not' is added to the verb itself, e.g. **aldım** 'I took' — **almadım** 'I did not take,' **sakhla!** 'stop!' — **sakhlama!** 'don't stop!' **Deyil** is also used, but as a separate word.

ESSENTIAL VERBS

The verb 'to be' is expressed in a variety of ways. The most common form you will find is the simple series of present endings:*

SINGULAR	PLURAL
-äm I am	**-ik** we are
-sän you are	**-siniz** you are
-dir he/she/it is	**-dir(lär)** they are

e.g. **Män hazıram.** 'I am ready.' (literally: 'I ready am.')

The verb 'to have' is also expressed in a variety of ways. The most common form you will encounter are **var/vardır** 'there is/are' and **yokh/yokhdur** 'there is/are not' — which are used with the possessive endings, e.g.

Mänim 25 yashım vardır. 'I am 25 years old.'
(literally: 'To me 25 my years there are.')
Mänim mashınım var. 'I have a car.'
(literally: 'To me my car there is.')

---

* Other forms in full are: **-am, -san, -dır/dür/dur, -ıq, -sınız/sünüz/sunuz, -dır(lar)/dür(lär)/dur(lar)**

PRONUNCIATION GUIDE

Azerbaijani letter	Azerbaijani example	Approximate English equivalent
a	**ana** 'mother'	c*a*r
ä	**män** 'I'	*a*pple
b	**bäli** 'yes'	*b*ox
ch	**chay** 'tea'	*ch*urch
d	**dagh** 'mountain'	*d*og
e	**ev** 'house'	p*e*t
f	**futbol** 'soccer'	*f*at
g	**gömrük** 'Customs'	Ma*gy*ar
gh	**maghaza** 'shop'	—
h	**häftä** 'week'	*h*at
i	**ish** 'work'	s*ea*t
ı	**qısh** 'winter'	—
j	**jaz** 'jazz'	*j*et
k	**kino** 'cinema'	*k*ick
kh	**kheyr** 'no'	lo*ch*, as in Scottish English
l	**ulduz** 'star'	*l*et
m	**mashın** 'car'	*m*at
n	**neft** 'oil'	*n*et
o	**ofis** 'office'	c*o*t
ö	**söz** 'word'	—
p	**prezident** 'president'	*p*et
q	**qiymät** 'price'	*g*ot
r	**radio** 'radio'	*r*at, but 'rolled' as in Scottish English
s	**su** 'water'	*s*it
sh	**shähär** 'town'	*sh*ut
t	**täyyarä** 'airplane'	*t*en
u	**buz** 'ice'	sh*oo*t
ü	**ünvan** 'address'	—
v	**vakht** 'time'	*v*an

y	**yol** 'road'	**y**es
z	**zälzälä** 'earthquake'	**z**ebra
zh	**zheton** 'token'	era**z**ure
'	**mä'na** 'meaning'	—

Since the object of this book is to help with speaking, an easy-to-read system of letters has been used to help with instant pronunciation. A key to the new Azerbaijani Roman alphabet, together with its Cyrillic predecessor, can be found on page 17. All words found in this book may be easily transliterated back into this key.

Nothing beats listening to a native speaker, but the following notes should help give you some idea of how to pronounce the following letters.

VOWELS

Note that vowels are always pronounced separately of each other but with a smooth join of the sounds, e.g. **saat** — 'sa-at', **majmuä** — 'majma-ä', **tabii** — 'tabi-i'.

ı   has a similar sound to the vowels in 'her' or 'stir' mixed up with the 'i' in 'peer' or 'fear'.

The following vowels are 'umlauted', and have similar pronunciation to German or Turkish ä, ö and ü:

ä   is like the 'a' in 'pat', but with a quality closer to 'pet' than 'part'.

ö   has a similar sound to the vowels in 'her' or 'stir', but without any 'r' and with pointed and narrowly rounded lips.

ü   has a similar sound to the vowel in 'huge' but much shorter. Another way of producing this is to say 'kiss' but with pointed and narrowly rounded lips, so that the 'i' almost becomes a 'u'.

CONSONANTS

gh is pronounced like a sort of growl in the back of your throat—like when you're gargling. The German or Parisian 'r' is the easy European equivalent. [= Arabic غ]

kh is the rasping 'ch' in Sottish 'loch' and German 'ach'. It is also pronounced like the Spanish/Castillian 'jota'. [= Arabic/Persian خ]

r varies between two forms: from the rolled Scottish variant, to a lightly breathed tap of the tongue that sometimes sounds similar to **zh**. This is the same **r** found in Turkish and Persian.

' is what is called the 'glottal stop'. In Azerbaijani, when it comes before a consonant, it prolongs the preceding vowel, often with a slight 'creak' of breath separating the two, e.g. **mä'na** is pronounced **'mä'äna,' she'r** as **'she'er.'** When it comes after a consonant, it is usually pronounced as a sort of stop or catch in the flow of breath before articulatingthe following vowel, e.g. **sur'ät** is pronounced **'sür-'ät.'** [= Turkish **'**/Persian ع]

NOTES

1) In many cases there are alternations of **q, k, gh** or **g** without change of meaning.

2) Consonants can be 'doubled', e.g. **gözällik** 'beauty' is pronounced very distinctly as **'gözäl-lik,' yeddi** '70' as **'yed-di.'**

3) Note that **h**, as a separate letter, is always pronounced in combinations like **mahnı** ('mah-nı'), **mäshhur** ('mäsh-hur').

4) Remember to make the distinction between **q** and **g**. It may help to think of **q** as being always 'hard' (as in 'got'), while **g** is always 'soft' (as in 'Magyar'), e.g. the town **Gänjä** is pronounced in a similar way to **'Gyänjä.'** Although not written, **k** too can sometimes be pronounced as **ky.**

THE AZERBAIJANI LATIN ALPHABET

(in use since 1991)

Azerbaijani letter	Transcription in this book	Name of letter	Azerbaijani letter	Transcription in this book	Name of letter
A a	[a]	a	N n	[n]	ne
B b	[b]	be	O o	[o]	o
C c	[j]	je	Ö ö	[ö]	ö
Ç ç	[ch]	che	P p	[p]	pe
D d	[d]	de	Q q	[g]	ge
E e	[e]	e	R r	[r]	re
Ə ə	[ä]	ä	S s	[s]	se
F f	[f]	fe	Ş ş	[sh]	she
G g	[g]	gye	T t	[t]	te
Ğ ğ	[gh]	ghe	U u	[u]	u
H h	[h]	he	Ü ü	[ü]	ü
İ i	[i]	i	V v	[v]	ve
I ı	[ı]	ı	X x	[kh]	khe
J j	[zh]	zhe	Y y	[u]	ye
K k	[k]	ke	Z z	[z]	ze
L l	[l]	le	'	[']	apostrof
M m	[m]	me			

THE AZERBAIJANI CYRILLIC ALPHABET

(in use since 1958)

Azerbaijani letter	Transcription in this book	Name of letter	Azerbaijani letter	Transcription in this book	Name of letter
A a	[a]	a	O o	[o]	o
Б б	[b]	be	Ө ө	[ö]	ü
В в	[v]	ve	П п	[p]	pe
Г г	[g]	ge	Р р	[r]	re
Ғ ғ	[gh]	ghe	С с	[s]	se
Д д	[d]	de	Т т	[t]	te
Е е	[e]	e	У у	[u]	u
Ә ә	[ä]	ä	Ү ү	[ü]	ü
Ж ж	[zh]	zhe	Ф ф	[f]	fe
З з	[z]	ze	Х х	[kh]	khe
И и	[i]	i	h h	[h]	he
Ы ы	[ı]	ı	Ч ч	[ch]	che
Ј ј	[y]	ye	Ҹ ҹ	[j]	je
К к	[k; ky]	ke	Ш ш	[sh]	she
К̡ к̡	[gy]	gye	'	[']	apostrof
Л л	[l]	el			
М м	[m]	em			
Н н	[n]	en			

AZERBAIJANI
DICTIONARY

AZERBAIJANI-ENGLISH
AZÄRBAYJANJA-İNGİLİSJÄ

A

ä'la excellent
-ä/-yä into
Abkhaz Abkhaz
Abkhazya Abkhazia
achar key; spanner
achıq *adjective* open
achmaq open; undo
ad name; **Adınız nädir?** What is your name?; **Adım Freddir.** My name is Fred.
ädäbiyyat literature
ädalät justice
adamlar people
adapter adapter
adät *tradition* custom
adatän usually
ad günü birthday
adi ordinary
Ädliyyä Nazirliyi Ministry of Justice
administrator administrator
admiral admiral
advokat lawyer
aeroport airport
aeroport vergisi airport tax
äfsänä legend
ägär if
agh white
agh jiyär lung
agh-qara plyonka B&W (film)
aghaj tree
aghajlıq wood; forest
aghılsız thick
aghır heavy
aghır qısh severe winter
aghız mouth
aghız üchün qar-qara därmanı mouthwash
aghjaqanad mosquito
aghlamaq weep
aghrı pain
aghrıkäsän därman painkiller
aghrıkäsän därmanlar painkillers
aghsakkal *noun* elder; village elder
ähali people; population
ähämiyyät significance
ähäng lime

ähvalat adventure *story*
ailä family
ailä väziyyäti marital status
äjaib strange
ajı bitter
ajımaq: Män ajımısham. I'm hungry.
ajiqli annoyed
äjnäbi foreigner
äjzachıkhana pharmacy
akademiya academy
akhın stream
akhırınjı last
akhmaq fool; silly; leak
akhsham evening
akhsham vakhtı p.m.
akhshamın(ız) kheyır! good evening!
akhtarısh exploration
akhtarmaq look for; search; seek
äkin planting
äkin sahäläri crops
äkizlär twins
äksinä opposite
aktyor actor
akumulyator battery
äl hand; arm; wrist
alabash sheepdog
älaqä connection
älätlär tools
älavä extra
älavä etmäk add
älavä yorghan an extra blanket
äl-ayaq limbs
älbattä certainly; of course
alcha sour plum
alchaq short; low
äl chantası handbag
äleyküm salam! hello! (*reply to* salam äleyküm!)
älifba alphabet
äl ishi handicraft
älil disabled
alıshqan lighter; **Alıshqan varmı?** Do you have a light?
alıshqan yanajaqı lighter fluid
äljäk gloves
alkohol alcohol
Allah God

allergiya allergy; **Mänim . . . qarshı allergiyam var.** I'm allergic to . . .
älli fifty
alma apple
Alman German *people*
Almaniya Germany
Almanja German *language*
almaq buy; receive; get
alo! hello! *on the phone*
äl radiosu walkie-talkie
älsilän napkin
äl televizoru portable TV
altı six
altında under *prep*
altınjı sixth
altmısh sixty
alt paltar underwear
ämäkdashlıq cooperation
Amerika America
Amerika Birläshmish Shtatları (=A.B.Sh.) U.S.A.
Amerikalı American
ämi uncle
ämin sure *adjective*
amputasiya amputation
ämr order *noun*
ämr etmäk order *someone*
an moment
ana mother
anadan olan gün date of birth
anadan olan yer place of birth
anadan olma birth
analiz analysis
än'änä tradition
än'änävi traditional
än azı at least
anbar store
anbar kiliti padlock
än böyük greatest
än chokh most
and ichmäk swear an oath
anesteziyachı anesthetist
anket form *official*
anlamaq realize:
anqar hangar
antibiotik antibiotic
antibiotiklär antibiotics
antifriz anti-freeze
antiseptik antiseptic
än yakhshı best
aparıjı qatar locomotive
aparmaq carry; to lead
apendisit appendicitis
Aprel April
aptek pharmacy

aqronom agronomist
är husband
äräb Arab
araba cart
äräbjä Arabic *language*
aragh arak; vodka
arashdırmaq investigate
arasında between
arasından through
ärazi region; territory; district
ärazi kodu (indeksi) area code
ärdä female
ärdäyäm: Män ärdäyäm. *female* I am married.
arı bee
ärimäk dissolve; thaw
arkha back; bottom
arkhada behind
arkheologiya archeology
arkheolozhi archeological
arkhitektura architecture
armud pear
arpa barley
artileriya artillery
artıq already
artıq baqazh excess baggage
artırmaq add
arvad wife
arzulamaq desire *verb*
as just
äsäb nerve
äsäbli angry
äsas main; reason
. . . äsasän according to
äsas qan damarı artery
äsas qanun constitution
äsası qoymaq found *verb*
ashaghı below; down; low
ashaqı qan täzyiqi low blood pressure
ashırım mountain pass
ashpaz cook *noun*
äsir hostage; prisoner
äskär soldier
äsl real
asmaq hang
aspirin aspirin
astma asthma
astmalı asthmatic
ät meat
at horse
ata father
ätäk lap
at sürmäk ride a horse
at yarıshı horse-riding

ät dükanı butcher's
atanızın adı middle name
atäsh achmaq shoot
atäsh achmayın! don't shoot!
atäshkäs ceasefire
atılmaq leap
ätir perfume
atlas atlas
atletika athletics
avadanlıq equipment
Avar Avar
avara unemployed
avariya accident; crash; emergency
avariya chıkhıshı emergency exit
äväzinä instead
aviapocht air mail
avqust August
Avropa Europe
Avropa İttifaqı European Union
Avropalı European *adjective*
Avstraliya Australia
Avstraliyalı Australian
avtobus bus
avtobus dayanajaghı bus stop
avtomat submachine gun
avtomobil car
avtomobil dayanajaqı car park
avtor author
avtovaghzal bus station
ävvälär previously
ävväli beginning
ay month; moon
ayagha qalkhmaq to get up; to wake up
ayaghyolu toilet(s)
ayaq foot
ayaq khizäyi idmanı skiing
ayaqqabı shoes
ayaqqabı dükanı shoeshop
aydın clear *adjective*
ayghır stallion
ayı bear
äyilmäk lean
ayıq awake
äymäk bend *verb*
äyyash alcoholic
äyyashlıq alcoholism
az not much; under
azad free
azad etmä liberation
azad etmäk release
azadlıq freedom
Azärbayjan Azerbaijan
Azärbayjanlı Azerbaijani
Azärbayjanja *language* Azerbaijani

az-chokh more or less
azlıq minority
azqala nearly

B

bä'zän sometimes
bä'zi some
baba grandfather
bädän body
bädbäkht unfortunate
bädbäkhtlikdän unfortunately
artıgh baqazh excess baggage
bagh garden
bagh orchard
Baghıshla! *familiar* Sorry!
baghıshlama *noun* excuse
Baghıshlayın! excuse me!
baghlama parcel; package; backpack; tow rope
baghlamaq shut; close; tie (up)
baghlı closed
baha expensive
bähräli fertile
bajarmaq to be able
bajı sister
bak tank; container
bakhmaq look
Bakı Baku
bakteriya bacteria
bal honey
balaja little; small
balaja televizor portable TV
bal ayı honeymoon
balet ballet
bäli yes
balıq fish
balıq ovu fishing
bälkä maybe; perhaps
Balkar Balkar
balkon balcony
balqabaq pumpkin
balta ax
bamper fender; bumper
bank bank
banka can *noun*
bank chekläri travelers' checks
banket banquet
bank ishchisi banker
bänövshäyi purple
baqazh baggage
baqazh bölmäsi baggage counter
baqazh yeri boot
bar bar
bärä ferry

bärabär together
barak barracks
baräsindä about
bärbär hairdresser
bärbärkhana barber's
barıshıq truce
bärk hard; loud
bärk soyuq freezing
bärkitmäk fix
barmaq finger
barmen bartender
barsız barren
bäsdir! that's enough!
basdırmaq bury
bash aghrısı headache
basha düshmäk understand
bash head
bashaltı pillow
bäshäri *adjective* human
bashchı chief
bash käläm cabbage
bashlamaq begin
bash meydan main square
bash nazir prime minister; premier
. . . bashqa except (for . . .)
bash vermäk happen
basketbol basketball
bästäkar composer
bataghlıq swamp
batareya battery
batmaq *verb* sink
bayat stale
bayır *adjective* outside
bayqush owl
bayram holiday
baza base
bazar ertäsi Monday
bazar market; Sunday
bazis basis
bel aghrısı backache
bel back *noun*
belä so
benzin gas; petrol
besh five
beyin sarsıntısı concussion *medical*
beynälkhalq kod international code
beynälkhalq operator international operator
beynälkhalq uchush international flight
bibär capsicum; sweet pepper
bıchaq knife
bichin reaping
bifshteks steak
bıgh mustache

bilmäk to be able; **Biz od qalaya bilärikmi?** May we light a fire?
bilet ticket
bilet kassası ticket office
bilgisayar computer
bilik knowledge
bilmäk know
bina building
bioqrafiya biography
bir one; **bir az** a little bit; **bir basha bilet** one-way ticket; **bir chokh** many; **bir däfä** once; **bir nechä** several; **bir pachka siqaret** carton of cigarettes; **bir shey** something; **bir yerdä** somewhere
birbasha direct
birdän-birä suddenly
birinji first
birinji klas first class
birisi gün the day after tomorrow
birisi someone/somebody
birläshdirmä unification
birläshmäk unite
Birläshmish Millätlär Täshkilatı United Nations
birläshmish united
birlikdä together
birtäräfli bilet one-way ticket
birtäräfli häräkat küchäsi one-way street
bishirmäk cook; bake
bit flea; louse
bitki plant
bitlär fleas
biz we
bizim our; ours
biznes business
biznes klass business class
biznesmen businessman/woman
blank form *official*
blyuz blues
B.M.T.-nin İnkishaf Proqramı UNDP
B.M.T.-nin Qachqınlar Üzrä Komisarlığı UNHCR
bochka barrel
boghaz throat
boghaz aghrısı sore throat
boghulmaq choke
böhran crisis
boks boxing
bölgä region
bölmä section
bölmäk divide
bölüshmäk share *verb*
bomba bomb

bombaları zärärsizläshdirmä bomb disposal
bombardman bombardment
bombardman täyyarä bomber
boran sleet
borj debt
borj almaq borrow
borj vermäk lend
boru pipe *tube*
bosh empty
boshaltmaq to desert
boshaltmaq to empty
boshanmısh divorced
boshqab plate
bosh vakht free time
boss boss; head
boya *noun* paint
boyamaq *verb* paint
boy atmaq grow
boylu pregnant
boylu pregnant; **Män boyluyam.** I'm pregnant.
böyräk kidney
böyük big; great
böyük barmaq thumb
böyümäk grow up
boyun neck
boyunbaghı necklace
böyürtkän wild strawberry
böyütmäk to breed
brendi brandy
Britaniya Britain
Britaniyalı British
brosh brooch
bu this
bu akhsham tonight
bud leg
Budda dini Buddhism
budda dindarı Buddhist
buddist Buddhist
budur ... here is ...
bugün today; this afternoon
bu häftä this week
bu il this year
büjä budget
bujaq angle
bu kimi like this
bu kimi such
bükülmüsh wrapped
bulaq suyu spring *water*
bu lazımdır it's necessary
bulka loaf
bulud cloud
buludlu cloudy
büllur crystal

bu nädir? what's that?
bundan ävväl ago
bundan bashqa also
bundan bashqa besides
bunlar these
bunlardır ... here are ...
bununla belä however
bura(ya) this way
burada here
burakhmaq release
burghu corkscrew
bürj tower
bürokratism bureaucracy
burun nose
buruq derrick
buterbrod sandwich
bütün whole
bütün; här all
bu yakhında soon
buyurunuz! please!
buz ice
buz baghlama solstice
buz baltası ice ax

C

domkrat *car* jack
buzov calf *(cow)*
chadır tent
chährayı pink
chakhir wine
chäki weight
chäkij hammer
chäkmäk pump *verb*
chäkmälär boots
chalmaq play *(a musical instrument)*
chälläk barrel
chamadan suitcase
chänä chin; jaw
chanaq sümüyü pelvis
chängäl fork
chanta bag
chäpär fence
chap etmäk print
chap mashını typewriter
char tsar
chärkäs Circassian
chärshänbä Wednesday
chärshänbä akhshamı Tuesday
chätin difficult; hard *(difficult)*
chätir umbrella
chatmamaq lack *verb*
chay qashıghı teaspoon
chay river; tea
chaynik kettle

chay sahili riverbank
Chechen Chechen
Chechenistan Chechnya
chek check *(money)*; **bank chekläri** travelers' checks
chevik rapid; rapidly
chevrä shape
cheynämäk chew
chıdır horse racing
chıgh avalanche
chıghırmaq shout; cry
chıkhartmaq take-out
chıkhısh exit
chimärlik beach
chimmäk bathe
Chin Chinese
chirkin; chirkli dirty
chiy raw
chiyäläk strawberry
chiyin shoulder
choban shepherd
chobaniti sheepdog
chokh deyil not much
chokh gözäl fine *adverb*
chokh much; very; too; **bir chokh** many
chokhdan for a long time
chokhluq majority
chokh pis worse
chökmä landslide
chör-chöp firewood
chöräk bread
chöräkkhana bakery
chöräk maghazası baker's
chovdar wheat
chughundur beetroot
chünki because

D

-da/-dä in; on
däb fashion
daban toe
dad taste
dadlı tasty
dadmaq to taste
dadsız tasteless
däfä time; **iki däfä** two times
däfnetmä märasimi funeral
däftärkhana lävazimatı stationery
däftärkhana malları maghazası stationer's
dagh mountain
dagh ätäyi foothills
daghın döshü slope

daghıntılar ruins
Daghıstan Daghestan
Daghıstanlı Daghestani
daghıtmaq scatter; destroy
Daghlıq Qarabagh Nagorno-Karabakh
dagh yolu mountain pass
daha . . . -er/-est; already; **daha balaja/kichik** smaller/smallest; **daha böyük** bigger/biggest
daha az less
daha bir another
daha chokh more
daha gänj junior
daha ujuz cheaper
daha yakhshı better
daha yashlı senior
dähshätli terrible
daim always
dairä circle
dakhil olmaqla (dakhil edilmish) included
dakhili interior
Dakhili Íshlär Nazirliyi Ministry of Home Affairs
dakhili uchush internal flight
dal bottom
dal ötürüjüsü reverse *adjective*
dalgha wave
dalghıj diver
däli crazy
dalında after
dalınja düshmäk chase
dälläk hairdresser
dälläkkhana barber's
dam roof
damba dam
dämir metal
dämir pulu coins
dämir yolu railway
dämir yolu stansiyası railway station
dämir yolu stansiyası train station
-dan/-dän from; than
. . .-dän bäri since
danimarka dilindä Danish
danıshıq conversation
danıshıqları aparan shäkhs negotiator
danıshmaq talk; **Siz Íngilisjä danıshırsınızmı?** Do you speak English?
däniz donanması navy
däniz sea
dänizdä offshore
däqiq exact; certainly

däqiqä minute *(of time)*
dar narrow
dara riot
daragh comb; hairbrush
därgi magazine
därhal direct
darı millet
däri leather; skin
därin deep
därin sular üchün platforma deep water platform
därman drug; medication
därs lesson
dartmaq draw; pull
darvaza gate
därzi dressmaker
dash rock; stone
dashımaq freight *verb*
dashqın flood
däsmal towel
däsmallar tissues
dästäk; dästäy handle; handset
dävä camel
davam etmäk to last
dä'vätnamä invitation
dä'vät olunmush mä'ruzächi guest speaker
davranısh etiquette
däyänäk *noun* stick
dayanmaq stay
däyär worth
dayı uncle
däyirman mill
däyishmä exchange; **Däyishmä dayari nä qädärdir?** What's the exchange rate?
däyishmäk replace; alter
dekabr December
demäk say; tell
demäk olar ki nearly
demokratik democratic
demokratiya democracy
deodorant deodorant
depo depot
deportasiya deportation
derivativ derivative
desert dessert
deshik hole; puncture
deyäsän likely
deyil not
diabet diabetes
diabet khästäsi diabetic
diaqnoz diagnosis
dib bottom
digär other

diktator dictator
diktatorluq dictatorship
dil tongue; language
dilchi linguist
dilchilik linguistics
din religion
dinamo dynamo
dinjälmäk relax
diplomat diplomat
diplomatik älaqälär diplomatic ties
diri alive
dırnaq fingernail
dırnaq qaychisi nail-clippers
dirsäk elbow
dish tooth
dish agrısı toothache
dish häkimi dentist
dish pastası toothpaste
dish shötkası toothbrush
dish üchün chöp toothpick
dishlämäk bite
dishlär teeth
disk zhokey disk jockey
disko disco
div giant
divar wall
diyeta diet
diyirjäkli qäläm ballpoint
diz knee
diz chökmäk kneel
dizel diesel
dodaq lip
dodaq pomadası lipstick
doghmaq to give birth to
doghum birth
doghum yeri place of birth
dokhsan ninety
dolab cupboard
dolar dollar
doldurmaq fill; **formanı doldurmaq** fill in a form
dolu full
don *noun* dress
dondurma ice cream
donmush ällär/ayaqlar frostbitten hands/feet
döngä bend *in road*
donma frostbite
dönmäk turn
donmaq freeze
donuz pig; pork
doqquz nine
dörd four
dörd yol aghzı crossroads
dörddäüch three-quarters

dörddäbir one-quarter
dördünjü fourth
döshäk mattress
döshämä floor
dost friend
dövlät nation; state
dövlät bashchısı head of state
dövlät chevrilishi coup d'état
dovshan rabbit
doymaq: Män doymusham. I'm full up!
döyüshchü fighter
döyüshmäk fight
dözmäk stand
drenazh drain
dua etmäk pray
dudkesh chimney
dükan shop
dükanchı shopkeeper
dul: Män dulam. I am widowed.
dul kishi widower
dul qadın widow
duluschu äshyaları pottery
duman smoke; fog; mist
dumanlı foggy; misty
dünän yesterday
dünya world
durbin binoculars
düriz scythe
durmaq rise
dush shower
düshärgä yeri campsite
düshmäk fall *verb*
düshmän enemy
düshmänchilik feud
düshünmäk think
düyü rice
duz salt
düz straight; straight on; **Düz sür.** Go straight ahead.
düz basha düshmämäk misunderstand
düzältmäk to correct
düzänlik *noun* plain
düzgün correct
duzlu salty

E

e'dam execution
ehtimal ki possible
ehtiyaj need; **Mänim ...-ä/a ehtiyajim var.** I need ...
ehtiyaj täkäri spare tire
ehtiyajı olmaq to (have a) need

ehtiyat hissäläri maghazası auto supply shop
ehtiyatlar reserves
ekspress express *fast*
elektrik electricity
elektrik düymäsi switch *(electric)*
elektrik gärginliyin nizamlayıjısı voltage regulator
elektrik jihazlar maghazası electrical goods store
elektrik spiral heating coil
elektron pochtu e-mail
elektron pochtu ünvanı e-mail address
elm science
elmi scientific; academic
elmi ishchi scientist; academic
Elmlär Akademiyası academy of sciences
e'mal etmäk refine
e'malatkhana refinery
enli thick; wide
epidemiya epidemic
epilepsiya epilepsy
epilepsiyalı epileptic
era era
Ermäni Armenian
Ermänijä Armenian *(language)*
Ermänistan Armenia
eshitmäk hear
eshshäk donkey
eshshäkarısı wasp
eskalator escalator
etiket etiquette
e'tiraz etmäk protest *verb*
e'tiraz protest *noun*
etmäk do; make
ev house
evlänmä marriage
evli: Män evliyam. I am married. *male*
eyds khästäliyi; spid khästäliyi AIDS
eyvan balcony
e'zamiyyät work

F

fäal activist
fabrika factory
fählä manual worker
fajiä disaster
faks fax
faks mashını fax machine
fäkt fact
familiya surname
fänär flashlight
färqli different

Fars Persian
Farscha Farsi
fäsil chapter; season
faydalı useful
fayl file *computer*
fe'l verb
federasiya federation
fen hairdryer
ferma farm
ferma täsärrufatchılığhı farming
fermer farmer
fevral February
fikir thought; idea; **fikrimjä ...** I think ...
film film; movie
filtrli filtered
filtrsiz filterless
final final *noun*
finans finance
fircha brush
finjan cup
fırtına storm
fizika physics
fizioterapiya physiotherapy
flash flash
folklor folklore
fond foundation *(organization)*
fonetika phonetics
forma form; **formanı doldurmaq** fill in a form
forum forum
fotoaparat camera
fotokamera avadanlığhı camera equipment
fotoqrafiya photography
fotosänät photography
foto shäkil photo
fotosürät photocopy
frank franc
Fransız French *(person)*
Fransızja French *(language)*
freyt freight
funt pound
funt sterlinq sterling
furqon van
fut foot *(measurement)*
futbol football; soccer
futbol matchı soccer match

G

gäläjäk future
gälän coming; **gälän häftä** next week; **gälän ildän sonra** the year after next
gälin ichäri! come in!

gälinjik doll
gälinjik weasel
gälish arrivals
gälish tarikhi date of arrival
gälmä stranger
gälmäk come; arrive
galyanaltı snack
gämi boat; ship
gamısh bull
gänj young person
gätirmäk bring
gavali plum
gedish tarikhi date of departure
gedishlär departures
gejä night; **gejän(iz) kheyrä qalsın!** good night!
gejä klubu nightclub
gejä yarısı midnight
gejikmä delay
gejikmäk to be late; **Täyyärä gejikir.** The plane is delayed.
gejikmish late
general general
genish wide
genishländirmäk extend
geoloq geologist
geri chäkmäk withdraw
geriyä backwards
getmäk go
geyinmäk to get dressed
geymäk wear
gid guide
gigiyena hygiene
gilämeyvä berry
ginekolog gynecologist
girish entrance
girish gadaghandır no entry
girmäk enter
girov götürän kidnapper
gizlätmäk hide
gizli *adjective* secret
gödän stomach
gohum-äqräbä relatives
goja old
göl lake
gömrük customs; customs duty
göndärmäk send
... görä according to
görkäm view
görmäk see
görmäyä getmäk visit
görünmäk look; appear
görüsh meeting
görüshmäk meet
göstärmäk to show

götürmäk take
göy sky; bruise
göy gurultusu thunder
göyärtisatan greengrocer
göz eye
göz yashı tear (of eye)
gözäl beautiful; good; fine
gözällik beauty
gözlämäk wait; wait for; expect
gözlanilmäz unexpected
gözlük glasses; eyeglasses
gözyashardıjı qaz tear gas
grammatika grammar
güdmäk watch
güjlü strong
gül flower
gül dükanı florist
güläsh wrestling
gülmäk laugh
güllä bullet
güllä sachan machine gun
güllä tower
gümüsh silver
gün day; bu gün today; sıragha gün
    the day before yesterday
gündür? What date is it today?
günahsız innocent
günäsh sun
günäsh shualarına qarshı krem
    sunblock cream
günäshli sunny; günäshlidir it is
    sunny
günbatan sunset
gündoghan sunrise
gündüz daytime
günorta noon; gunortan(ız) kheyir!
    good afternoon!
günortadan sonra afternoon
Gürjü Georgian (people)
Gürjü dilindä Georgian (language)
Gürjüstan Georgia
güzgü mirror

H

hä yes
häb pill; tablet
häbs düshärgäsi concentration camp
häbs etmäk arrest
häbskhana prison
hädäf goal; aim
hädd limit; häddindän artıgh az too
    little; häddindän artıgh chokh
    too many/much
hädiyyä gift; present

hädiyyälär maghazası souvenir shop
häftä sonu weekend
häftä week; bu häftä this week;
    gälän häftä next week; kechän
    häftä last week
hajı pilgrim to Mecca
häjm size (quantity)
häkim doctor
hakim judge; referee
hal state; condition
hälä still; yet
hälä yokh not yet
hälä ki until
häll etmäk solve
hämail necklace
hamam otaghı bathroom
hamam Turkish baths
hamburger hamburger
hämchinin also
hamilä pregnant
hamiläliyin qashısını alan tädbirlär
    birth control
hämishä always
hämishäki usual
hämkar colleague
hämkarlar ittifaqı trade union
hämlä attack; ambush
hämlä etmäk to attack
hansı? which?
hansı növdän? what kind?
häqiqät fact; truth
häqiqi true; actual
haqlı right; Siz haqlısınız! You are
    right!; Siz haqlı deyilsiniz! You're
    wrong!
haqq (human) right
här each; every
harada? where?; ... haradadır?
    where is ...?; ... haradadırlar?
    where are ...?
haradan? where from?
härarät temperature
harasa somewhere
härbi military
härbi äsir P.O.W.
härbi äsirlär düshärgäsi P.O.W. camp
härbi hava donanması airforce
härbi jinayät war crime
härbi tribunal war tribunal
här birisi anyone
härchänd although
här gün every day
här iki(si) both
här ... ikisi both ... and
här käs anyone; everybody; everyone

härlätmäk spin
härshey everything
häsharat insect
hava air; weather
hava hüjumu air raid
hava limani airport
hava qüvväläri air force
hava yolları shirkäti airline
häyät yard *(distance)*
häyat life
hazır ready
hazırlamaq prepare
häzz pleasure
hech käs no one; nobody
hech nä nothing
hech vakht never
hech yerä nowhere
hekäyä story
helikopter helicopter
herik sahä fallowland
hesab bill; **Hesab nechä oldu?**
  What's the score?
hesabat report
heykäl statue
heyvan animal
Hind Indian
Hindistan India
hind toyughu turkey
Hindu dindarı Hindu
Hindu dini Hinduism
hindushka turkey
hipertoniya high blood pressure
hipotoniya low blood pressure
hiss sense
hiss etmäk feel
hissä chapter
hissä part
hissiyyat feeling
hökmdar ruler *person*
hökmranlıq reign *noun*
hökumät government
hollandiyalı Dutch
hörümchäk spider
hovuz pool; swimming pool
hövzä basin
hüdud border; frontier
hüjum attack; raid
humanitar humanitarian
humanitar yardım humanitarian aid
humanitar yardım ishchisi aid
  worker
hüquq law
hüquqi legal
hüquqlar rights
hüquqshunas lawyer

hürmäk *verb* bark

I

ibadätgah shrine
ichäriyä in
Íchäri Shähär Old (Inner) City *(in
  Baku)*
ichki a drink
ichki düshkünü alcoholic
ichmäk to drink
ichmäli su drinking water
idarä board council
idkhal etmäk to import
idman sports
idmanchı athlete
ifa etmäk perform
ifadä etmäk to express
iftikhar pride
ijazä vermäk allow
ijlas session
ijma community
ijmal review *newspaper*
ijra etmäk execute
ikän while
ikhraj export *verb*
ikhrajat export *noun*
ikhtira invention
ikhtirachı inventor
iki two; **iki häftä** fortnight; **iki däfä**
  twice; **iki däfä artıq** double; **iki
  basha bilet** return ticket
ikinäfärlik otaq double room
ikinji *adjective* second
ikinji däräjä/klas second class
ikitäräfli bilet return ticket
il year; **bu il** this year; **gälän ildän
  sonra** the year after next; **kechän
  il** last year; **növbäti il** next year
ilan snake
ilan dishlämäsi snakebite
ilbiz snail
ilıgh warm
ilk yardım first aid
imam imam
imkansız impossible
imtahan exam
imza signature
imzalamaq to sign (an agreement)
inäk cow
inanmaq believe
indi now
indikator ishıqı indicator light
indiki *adjective* present
infeksiya infection

indiki

İngilis English
İngilisjä English *(language)*
İngiltärä England
İngush Ingush
injäsänät art
injäsänät qalereyası art gallery
inkishaf development
inqilab revolution
insan human being
insan hüquqlari human rights
insanlar people
insektisid insecticide
insha composition; essay
institut institute
internet Internet
interval interval
ipäk silk
iqtisadchi economist
iqtisadiyyat economics
irälidä before
irälilämäk forward *verb*
iräliyä forwards
İran Iran
İranlı Iranian; Persian
iri buynuzlu heyvanlar cattle
irinli septic
İrlandiya Ireland
İrlandiyali Irish
irtijachı reactionary
ish job; occupation; work
ishal diarrhea
isharä *noun* sign
ishchi worker; member of staff
ishchi heyyäti staff
ishgal occupation *(of a country)*
ishgalchı qüvvälär occupying forces
ishgänjä torture
ishgänjä vermäk to torture
ishghal invasion
ishıq light; electricity
ishıq güjünü ölchän jihaz light meter
ishıq jihazi lighting
ishıqlı light *(not dark)*
ishküzar adam businessman/
    businesswoman
ishküzar säfär business
ishlämäk to work; Telefon ishlämir.
    The phone doesn't work.
ishlänmish qazın chıkhması üchün
    boru exhaust; muffler *(of car)*
ishlänmish second-hand
ishlätmä use
ishsiz unemployed
ishsizlik unemployment
ishtirak etmäk participate

isim noun
isitmä fever; heating
İslam Islam
islatmaq to wet
İspaniyalı Spanish
İspanja Spanish *(language)*
İsrail Israel
istämäk want; wish
isti hot
isti su hot water
istila etmäk conquer
istilik dalghası heatwave
istilikölchän thermometer
istiot pepper
istiotlu hot *spicy*
istiotlu spicy *hot*
istiqamätlär directions
istirahät etmäk rest *verb*
istirahät rest *noun*
it dog
itälämäk push
İtaliya Italy
İtaliyalı; İtaliyan Italian *person*
İtalyanja Italian (language)
iti sharp
itirmishmäk lose; Män otaghımın
    acharını itirmishäm. I have lost
    my key.; Män yolumu itirmishäm.
    I am lost.
ittifaq unification; union
ittiham etmäk *legal* accuse
iy vermäk stink *verb*
iyirmi twenty
iynä needle; syringe
İyul July
İyun June
izahat explanation
izah etmäk explain

J

jädväl timetable
jähännäm hell
jähd etmäk try
jalashdırmaq put through on the
    phone
jalashdırmaq transfer on the
    phone
jäld *quick* fast
jällad executioner
jamaat people; folk
jämiyyät society
Jänäb Mr.

janavar wolf
jännät paradise
jänub south; southern
järrah surgeon
järrahiyyä ämäliyyatı operation; surgery
järrahiyyä ämäliyyatı otaghı operating theater
jäsäd copse
jäsur brave
jasus spy
javab answer
javab vermäk reply
javan young
jaz jazz
jäzalandırmaq punish
jib pocket
jib bıjaghı penknife
jib telefonu mobile phone
jiddi serious
jıghır path
jihaz appliances
jinayät crime
jinayätkar criminal
jinqil gravel
jinsi orqanlar genitals
jinsiyyät sex
jinz jeans
jip 4-wheel drive
jorab sock; **jorablar** socks
Jümä Akhshamı Thursday
Jümä Friday

K

käbab kebab
Kabardin Kabardian
kabel cable
kabinet cabinet
kafi satisfactory; sufficient
kaghız paper (substance)
kaghız pulu bank note(s)
kaha cave
kahı lettuce
käklik partridge
käläm cabbage
kalbasa sausage
kalkulyator calculator
Kalmık Kalmuk
kämär belt; rope
kamera camera
kämiyyät amount
känä tick (insect)
Kanada Canada
Kanadalı Canadian

kanal canal; channel
känd village; **känd yeri** in the country
kändli farmer
känd täsärrufatchısı farmer
känd täsärrufatı agriculture
Känd Täsärrufatı Nazirliyi Ministry of Agriculture
kanistra canister
käpänäk butterfly
kapital capital (finance)
kapot hood; bonnet (of car)
kar deaf
Karachay Karachai
karandash pencil
kärpich brick
kärtänkälä lizard
kartof potato
kärvan caravan
kaset (tape) cassette
käshf etmäk discover
käsishmä crossing
käsishmäk to cross
käsmäk cut; chop. **Isitmä käsilib.** The heating has been cut off.; **İshıq käsilib.** The electricity has been cut off.; **Qaz käsilib.** The gas has been cut off.; **Su käsilib.** The water has been cut off.; **Söhbätimi käsdilär.** I've been cut off.; **Khättlär käsilib.** The lines have been cut.
kassa cashier's booth
kassir cashier
katib male secretary
katibä female secretary
Katolik Catholic
kazino casino
kechän häftä last week
kechän il last year
kechi goat
kechid crossing
kechiriji transformer
kechmäk to pass
kechmish past
kechup ketchup
kemping camping
keramika ceramics
keshish priest
keyläshdiriji anesthetic
khäbär message; report
khäbärlär news
khäbärlär agentliyi news agency
khachpäräst Christian
khachpärästlik Christianity
khain treacherous, traitor

khalcha carpet; rug
khalq folk; nation; people
khalq musiqisi folk music
khalq räqsi folk dancing
kham neft crude oil
khämir flour
khämir yemäyi (garnir) pasta
Khanım Miss/Mrs./Ms.
khänjär dagger
khäräk stretcher
kharakter character
khärchäng cancer
khardal mustard
kharij etmä deportation
kharij etmäk deport
kharij olaraq excluded
kharijä out
khariji foreign
Khariji İshlär Nazirliyi Ministry of Foreign Affairs
khäritä map; **Bakının khäritäsi** map of Baku
khärjlämäk spend
kharrat carpenter
khäsarät trauma
khästä sick; *medical* patient; **Män khästäyäm.** I am sick.
khästäkhana clinic; hospital
khästälik disease; illness
khätkesh ruler *(measure)*
khätt line; cable; row
khäyanät etmäk betray
Khäzär Dänizi Caspian Sea
khäzinä treasury
kheyr no
kheyriyyächilik charity *(organization)*
khidmät service
khilas etmäk save
khırda pul loose change
khiyar cucumber
khizäk enishi ski slope
khor choir
khoräk däsmalı napkin
khoruz rooster
khosh: khosh gälmisän! /khosh gälmishsiniz! welcome!
khoshbäkht happy
Khristian Christian
Khristianlıq Christianity
khudahafiz! good-bye!
khumarlıq hangover
khüsusilä especially
ki *conjunction* that
kibrit matches
kichik little; small

kifayät: bu kifayätdir! that's enough!
kifayät deyil not enough
kifayätdir enough
kilid doorlock; lock
kilim kilim
kilometr kilometer
kiloqram kilogram
kilsä church
kim? who?
kimi as; like
kimsä someone/somebody
kimyä chemistry
kimyävi chemical
kino the movies
kino ishchisi filmmaker
kinoteatr cinema
kiosk kiosk
kirayä etmäk hire
kirkha cathedral
kisä sack
kishi male; man
kitab book
kitab maghazası bookshop
kitabcha notebook
kitabkhana library
klassik musiqi classical music
klinika clinic
kloun clown
klub club
kobud rude
köchmäk move
kod code
köhnä shähär old city
köhnä old; stale
köklmäk to get fat
kölgä shade
kolkhoz collective farm
kollej college
kömäk edini! Help!
kömäk etmäk *verb* help
komanda team
komissiya faizi commission; **Komissiya faizi nä qädärdir?** What is the commission?
kompakt disk CD
kompas compass
kompensasiya compensation
kompüter computer
kompüter chap mashını printer *computer*
komunikasiyalar communications
komunist communist
komunizm communism
kömür coal
kömür mä'däni coal mine

kondisioner air-conditioner; air-conditioning
konfrans conference
konfrans otağı conference room
konkı sürmäk skating
konsert concert
konsert zalı concert hall
konserva achan can opener
konslaqer concentration camp
konstitusiya constitution
konsulluq consulate
kontakt linzaları contact lenses
kontakt linzaları üchün tämizläyiji contact lens solution
konteyner container *freight*
kontrakt contract
kontrol control
konyak brandy; cognac
kopiya mashını photocopier
kor blind
körfäz bay
korlamaq spoil
körpä infant
körpü bridge
kosmetika make-up
kosmetika kabinäsı beauty parlor
kostyum suit
kotan plow
köynäk shirt
kral king; monarch; royal
kralicha queen
kran *mechanical* crane; faucet/tap
kredit credit
kredit kartı credit card
kreslo chair
kristal crystal
kseroks photocopier
kücha street
küläk wind *noun*
küläkli windy
külgabı ashtray
külüng pickax
Kumık Kumyk
küräk shoulder
Kürd Kurd
kurort spa
kürsü chair
kürü caviar
kuzov basket
kvartal housing estate/project; quarter

L

-la/-lä with
laboratoriya laboratory

läghv etmäk cancel
lähchä dialect
lak varnish
lakin but
lampa lamp; lightbulb
laptop kompüteri laptop computer
Laz Laz
Läzgi Lezgian
lazım: Mänä . . . lazımdır. I need . . .
lazımdır; bu lazımdır it's necessary
lazımi qädär right *amount*
läzzät pleasure
lentä yazmaq *verb* record
lider leader
lift elevator/lift
liman dock; harbour; port
linza lens
linzalar contact lenses
litr liter
lobya beans
lokomotiv locomotive
lumu lemon
lumulu chay tea with lemon

M

mä'bäd monument; temple
mädän mine *(mineral)*
mädäniyyät culture
mä'dä pozghunluqu indigestion
mä'dä yarası stomach ulcer
mädräsä madrasa
madyan mare
mafiya mafia
mäftil cable; wire
maghara cave
maghaza shop/store
maghazaları gäzmäk shopping
mäghlubiyyät defeat; failure
mäghrur proud
mähäbbät love
mähällä housing estate/project
mähkämä law court; *legal* trial
mahnı song
mahnı okhumaq sing
mähsul harvest; product
mähsul yetishtirmäk grow crops
mäjara adventure
mäjburi köchkün Displaced Person; Internally Displaced Person
mäjlis assembly; forum
mäjmüä review *newspaper*
mäkhfi polis secret police
mäktäb school
mäktub letter

mal äti beef
mäläfä sheet
-malı/-mäli have to
malik olmaq have; own
maliyya capital; finance
maliyyächi banker
mälumat information
mälumat bürosu information office
mama häkimi midwife
mämäl mammal
män I
mänä me
mä'na meaning
mä'nası olmaq to mean
mänbä origin; source
mäni me
mänim my
mänimki *adjective* mine
mantar cork; stopper
mänzärä sight; eyesight
mänzil apartment
mänzil-qärargah headquarters
mäqalä article; paper
maqnitli magnetic
maqnitofon tape-recorder
mäqsäd aim; **säfärin mäqsädi** reason for travel
maral deer
maraq interest
maraqlı interesting
marka *postal* stamp; mark *(currency)*
märkäz center
märmi shell *(military)*
Mart March
masa table; desk
mäsafä range
mäshhur famous; well-known
mashın car; vehicle; machine
mashının sänädläri car papers
mashınlara qarshı mina anti-vehicle mine
mäshq exercise
mäshqul: Siz nä ilä mäshqulsunuz? What do you do?; **O, mäshquldur.** The line is busy.
mäsjid mosque
mäskän accommodation
mäslähätchi consultant
mäsuliyyät charge
mätbäkh kitchen
mätbäkh böjäyi cockroach
mätbäkh sobası cooker
mätbuat media
material material
mätn text

mavzoley mausoleum
may May
mäzäli funny
mäzar grave; tomb
mä'zunniyyät vacation
me'mar architect
mebel furniture
mehmankhana hotel
mehriban kind *adjective*
mehtab full moon
mekhanik mechanic
me'marlıq architecture
mentollu menthol
menyu menu
meshä forest
metr meter
metro subway /underground/metro
meydan pitch; town square
meyit corpse
meyvä fruit
meyvä suyu fruit juice
mikrob germs
mikroskop microscope
mil mile
Milad Bayramı Christmas
millät nationality
Milli Mäjlis parliament *(of Azerbaijan)*
milli (etnik) tämizlämä ethnic cleansing
milyon million
min thousand
mina enamel; mine *(explosive)*
minalanmısh sahä minefield
minanı zärärsizläshdirmäk clear mines
mina qoymaq lay mines
mina tämizläyiji mine disposal
mina tapan mine detector
mina yatızdırmaq lay mines
minarä minaret
minaya düshmäk hit a mine
mineral mineral
mineral su mineral water
minnät: Chokh minnätdaram. I am grateful.
Minqrel Mingrelian
miqdar; nömrä number
mirvari pearl
mis copper
mishar *noun* saw
misharlamaq *verb* saw
mobil telefon mobile phone
moda fashion *(clothes)*
model model

modem modem
möhür *official* stamp
möjüzä miracle
molla mullah
monastır monastery
motosiklet motorbike
mövjud present *(time)*
mövsum season
mövzu subject
müalijä *noun* cure
müalija etmäk *verb* cure
müällim *male* teacher
müällimä *female* teacher
müasir contemporary; modern
müässis enterprise
müässisä factory
müäyyän certain
mübahisä dispute
mübarizä struggle
müdafiä etmäk defend
müdafiä etmäk maintain
Müdafiä Nazirliyi Ministry of Defense
müddät period
müddätindä during
müdir manager
müdriklik wisdom
mühafizächi guard *noun*
mühajir immigrant
mühajirät immigration
mühändis engineer
müharibä war
müharibä etmäk wage war
mühärrik engine
muhasib accountant
mühazirä lecture
mühit climate
mühüm important
mükafat prize
mükhalifät opposition
mukhtar autonomous
mukhtariyyat autonomy
mülki adam civilian
mümkündür probable; probably
mümkündürsä if possible
mümkünsä if possible
münasibät occasion
müqäddäs saint
müqäddäs yer shrine
müqäddimä introduction
müqayisä etmäk compare
müräkkäb ink
müsabiqä competition
müsahibä interview
müsälman Muslim
müshahidächi observer

müshayyät convoy
müshtük flint
musiqi music; **khalq musiqisi** folk music
musiqi yazısı record; L.P.
müstäqil independent
müstäqil dövlät independent state
müstäqillik independence
mütäkhässis professional
mütäkhässis specialist
müzakirä discussion
müzakirä etmäk discuss
muzdulu mercenary
muzey museum
mährum etmäk deprive

N

nä? what?; what kind?; **nä . . . nä** neither . . . nor; **nä qädär?** how many?; how much?; **nä qädär uzagh?** how far?; **nä qädär yakhın?** how near?; **nä vakht?** when?
näfärlik: bir näfärlik otaq single room
näfäs breath
näghmä song
nahar lunch
nahar etmäk to dine; to have lunch
Nakhchıvan Nakhichevan
nakhır flock
namä'lum unknown
nänä grandmother
naqil gear
Näqliyyat Nazirliyi Ministry of Transport
näqliyyat transport
narahat olmaq to be worried
narahat uncomfortable
narınjı orange *colour*
narkoman drug addict
nashir publisher
näshr etmäk publish
nasos pump
nasos mäntäqäsi pumping station
nätijädä as a result
nävä grandchild
näzakätli polite
nazik thin
nazir minister
nazirlik ministry
nechä?; nechä dänä? how many?
neft oil; petroleum
neft akhını oil spill
neftayırma müässisäsi oil refinery

neftchi oil worker
neft istehsalı oil production
neft kämäri oil pipeline
neft läkäsi oil slick
neft mä'däni oilfield
neft quyusu oil well
neft tankeri oil tanker
neft yataghı oilfield
nejä? how?
nejäsä somehow
nejäsiniz? how are you?
neytral neutral drive
nifrät etmäk hate
nishan mark
niyä? why?
niyyät etmäk intend
nömrä number
Noqay Nogai
normal normal; average
növ kind *noun*
növbäti il next year
növbäti next
Novruz New Year *(March 21)*
Noyabr November
nümayändä representative
nümayändälik representation
nümayish *political* demonstration
nümayishchilär *political* demonstrators
nümayish etmäk exhibit *verb*
nümunä example
nush olsun! bon appetit!
nuvä elektrik stansiyası nuclear
   power station
nüvä dövläti *political* nuclear power
nüvä qüvväsi nuclear power

O

o he; she; it; that
o biri other; rest
ödämä payment
ödämäk pay
odun firewood
ofis office
ofis ishchisi office worker
ofisiant waiter
oghlan boy
oghlan dostu boyfriend
oghru thief
oghul son
oghurlamaq steal; kidnap; **Mänim . . .
   oghurlanıb.** My . . . has been
   stolen.
oghurluq theft
öhdälik obligation

ojaq stove
okhshar similar
okhu reading
okhumaq read; study
o kimi like that
oksigen oxygen
Oktyabr October
ola bilär possible
olarmı? may I?
ölchmäk *verb* measure
ölchü size
öldürmäk kill; murder
ölkä country
ölmäk die
olmaq be; become
ölü dead
ölüm death
on ten
ona him; her; it; that
ona görä because of
on altı sixteen
on besh fifteen
on bir eleven
onda then
ondan sonra next to
on doqquz nineteen
on dörd fourteen
on iki twelve
onillik decade
onlar they; those
onların their; theirs
on säkkiz eighteen
onu him; her; it
onu da . . . bunu da both . . . and
onun his; her/hers; its
onun özü himself; herself; itself
on üch thirteen
onun qädärindä as much
onun üchün therefore
onunju tenth
onurgha spine *back*
on yeddi seventeen
opera opera
opera teatrı opera house
operator operator
öpmäk kiss
ora(ya) that way
orada there
orada var there is/are
ördäk duck
ordu army
orizhinal original
orta middle; average
ortasında among
Osetiya Ossetia

Osetiyalı Ossete
ösküräk cough
ot bitkisi grass; herb; hay
otaghın nömräsi room number
otaghı tämizlämä khidmäti room service
otaq room; **täk otaq/bir näfärlik otaq** single room; **iki näfärlik otaq** double room
otel hotel
oturajaq chair; seat
oturmaq sit
ötürüjü gear
otuz thirty
ov etmäk hunt
ovlamaq chase
oyatma zängi wake-up call
oyatmaq wake
oynamaq play; perform
öyränmäk learn; study
öyrätmäk teach
oyun game
öz(ünün) *adjective* own
özläri themselves
özü himself; herself; itself
özüm myself
özümüz ourselves
özünü-idarä self-rule

P

pab pub
padshah shah
paket package
pakhla beans
Pakistan Pakistan
Pakistanlı Pakistani
palchıq mud
palıd oak
paltar clothes; dress
paltar dükanı clothes shop
paltar geymäk put on clothes
paltarın yuyulması khidmäti laundry service
paltarkäsän dressmaker
paltartämizläyän laundry
paltaryuyan laundry
palto coat; overcoat
pambıgh cotton; cotton wool
pamidor tomato
pänjärä window
papagh hat
paralich olmaq paralyze
parashut parachute
park park

parlamaq shine
parlament parliament
parprez windshield
partiya game; match
partizan guerrilla
partlamamısh bomba unexploded bomb
partlamaq burst; explode; blow up
partlayıjı maddä explosives
partlayısh explosion
pas rust
pasient patient *(medical)*
Paskha Bayramı Easter
pasport passport
pasportun nömräsi passport number
pay portion
päyä barn
payachıq tent pegs
payız autumn/fall
paytakht capital city
pediatr pediatrician
pediatriya pediatrics
pendir cheese
penisilin penicillin
penjäk jacket
peshä profession
peyin fertilizer
peyk satellite
peyk telefonu satellite phone
piano piano
pilot pilot
piltä tampon
pilläkän stairs
pis bad; badly
pishik cat
pitsa pizza
pivä beer
piväkhana pub
piyadalara qarshı mina anti-personnel mine
plastır Band-Aid
plastmas plastic
platforma nömräsi platform number
platforma platform
plyazh beach
plyonka film *for camera*
pocht kartı postcard
pocht mail; post office
pocht qutusu mailbox
podval basement/cellar
poema poem
polad iron; steel
polis police
polis näfäri (ishchisi) policeman

polis shö'bäsi police station
politoloq political scientist
poni pony
portaghal orange
portret portrait
pozan eraser
pozmaq undo
pravoslav khristian Orthodox
premyer premier
prezervativ condom
prezident president; **vitse-prezident** vice-president
prezident qvardiyası presidential guard
prinsip principle
printer printer (computer)
priz prize
probkaachan corkscrew
problem problem
problem deyil! no problem!
professor professor
proqram program
protez artificial limb; prosthesis
proyektor projector
prozhektor flashlight
pub pub
pul money; currency
pul järimäsi fine of money
pulemyot machine gun
pul kisäsi wallet
pulsuz free of charge
pul yıghmaq save money
pusqu ambush noun
püstä pistachio
pyes play theater

Q

qabaq front
qabaghında in front of
qäbälik constipation
qabagha forward
qabaq shushä windshield
qabıgh shell (of nut)
qabiliyyät ability; skill
qabiliyyätli skilled
qäbiristanlıq cemetery
qäbz receipt
qachaqmalchı smuggler
qachmaq run; escape; flee
qachqın refugee
qachqınlar refugees
qachqınlar düshärgäsi refugee camp
qadagh nail
qadaghan veto

qadaghan edilmish forbidden
qadaghan etmäk forbid
qädär so much/many; **nä qädär?** how many?; **Bunu qiymäti nä qädärdir?** How much does this cost?; **Nä qädär vermäliyäm?** What is the charge?
qädim ancient
qadın woman; female
qadın jorabları tights
qadın ofisiant waitress
qäfädän kettle
Qafqaz Caucasus
Qafqaz Daghları Caucasus Mountains
qähräman character (in book etc.)
qähräman hero
qähvä coffee
qähväyi brown
qala castle; fort
qäläbä variety; victory
qäläm pen
qaldırıjı kran skilift
qaldırmaq lift; raise
qalkhmaq: Täyyarä nä zaman qalkhır? What time does the plane take off?
qalmaq remain
qalmaqal riot
qalon gallon
qälpä shrapnel
qalstuk tie/necktie
qälyan pipe (smoking)
qamıshlıq marsh
qämli sad; unhappy
qan blood
qänaät economy; saving
qan akhmaq bleed
qan chatıshmazlıqı anemia
qan köchürülmäsi blood transfusion
qan qrupu blood group
qan täzyiqi blood pressure
qanad wing
qanchır bruise
qänd sugar
qaneediji satisfactory
qanköchürmä blood transfusion
qanqrena gangrene
qanqster gangster
qapı door
qar snow; **qar yaghır** it is snowing
qara black
qara bazar black market
Qarachı Gypsy
qarajiyär liver

qara milchäk fly *(insect)*
qaranlıq dark; darkness
qärar decision
qärara gälmäk decide
qarätchilik robbery
qarazh garage
qärb west
qärbi west; western
qardash brother
qargha crow *(bird)*
qarghıdalı maize
qarghudalı corn
qarın stomach
qarın aghrısı stomachache
qarıshıq salmaq confuse
qarıshka ant; termite
qarlı boran blizzard
qarnizon garrison
qarpız watermelon
qarshılıq compensation
qashınma itch
qashıq spoon
qartal eagle
qar täpäsi snowdrift
qar uchghunu avalanche
qar yaghını snowdrift
qat floor *storey*
qatar train
qatıgh yogurt
qatil killer; murderer; assassin
qatır mule
qätl murder
qätlä yetirmäk *verb* murder
qatran gum
qavrama reception desk
qaya rock
qaychı scissors
qayghı care
qayghıchäkän careful
qayghısına qalmaq care
qayıtmaq return
qaynamaq *verb* boil
qaz gas; goose
qaz balonu gas bottle/canister
qäzet newspaper; İngilisjä qäzet
    newspaper in English
qäzet dükanı newsstand
qazıma drilling
qazıma mashını *noun* drill
qazımaq dig
qaz istehsalı gas production
qazlı sparkling
qaz pedalı accelerator
qaz quyusu gas well
qaz yataghı gas field

qeyd record *(document)*
qeydiyyat check-in
qeydiyyat bölmäsi check-in counter
qeydiyyat nömräsi car registration
qeyri-kafi not enough
qeyri-normal insane
qeyri-qanuni illegal
qıfıl padlock
qın sea-shell
qiqiyena lävazimatı toiletries
qırghın massacre
qırkh forty
qırmaq break; hook
qırmızı red
Qırmızı Khach Red Cross
Qırmızı Aypara Red Crescent
qısa chay fasiläsi break for
    refreshments
qısh winter
qıshın ortası midwinter
qıtlıq shortage
qiymät cost; price; Bunu qiymäti nä
    qädärdir? How much does this cost?
qız daughter; girl
qız dostu girlfriend
qızardılmısh kartof french fries
qızdırma temperature; Mänim qızdır-
    mam var. I have a temperature.
qızıl gold
qızıl gül rose
qoch ram
qohum relative
qohumluq relationship
qokhu smell
qol goal; lever; Kim qol vurdu? Who
    scored?
qolf golf
qol saatı watch; wristwatch
qolbagh bracelet
qonagh evi guesthouse
qonaghlıq party
qonaq guest; visitor
qonaq getmäk visit
qonshu neighbor
qorkhmaq to be afraid of
qorkhu fear
qorkhunj terrible
qorkhutmaq frighten
qorumaq guard; protect
qorunma protection
qoshqu clutch *of car*
qoshunlar troops
qovluq file *(paper)*
qovmaq expel
qöy blue

qöy qurshaghı rainbow
qoymaq lay; put
qoyun sheep
qoz nut; walnut
qram gram
qrip flu/influenza
qrup group
quduzluq rabies
qulaq asmaq listen
qulaq ear
quldur bandit; gangster
qum sand
qumarkhana casino
qumbara grenade
qunä qarshı eynäk sunglasses
Qur'an Koran
qurbagha frog
qurd därmani insecticide
qurd worm
qurghushun lead (metal)
qurmaq establish; wind up
qurtarmaq finish; run out; **Yanajaghım qurtarib.** I have run out of gas.
qurub sunset
qush bird
qüvvä power
qüvvät strength
quyu noun well
quyu qazımaq drill a well
quyu qazıma mä'däni well site
quzu lamb
qvardiya guard noun

R

rabitä communications
radar radar
radiator radiator
radio radio
radio stansiyası radio station
radio verilishi radio program
radio ötürüjüsü radio transmitter
radio yayımı radio broadcast
räf drawer
rahat comfortable
rähbär leader
rahib monk
rahibä nun
rähmsiz cruel
raket missile
Ramazan Bayramı Ramadan
rämz symbol
räng color
rängli plyonka color film
rängsiz colorless

räqämli digital
räqs dance; dancing; **khalq räqsi** folk
   dancing
räsm picture
räsmi geyim uniform
rässam artist; painter
ratusha city hall; town hall
rayon region; district
razetka (electric) plug
razı satisfied
razılashmaq yield
razılıq agreement
reallıq reality
redaktor editor
rekord record (sports)
rentgen X-ray
reparasiya reparation
reqbi rugby
respublika republic
restoran restaurant
reyd raid
rezhim regime
rezin rubber
risq risk
riyazıyyat mathematics
rok konserti rock concert
rok-end-rol rock 'n' roll
roman novel; **İngilisjä romanlar**
   novels in English
rüb quarter
rubl ruble
ruh soul
Rus Russian
Ruscha Russian (language)
rüshvätkhorluq corruption
Rusiya Russia
rüsümsüz tax-free

S

saat clock; hour; **saat nechädir?**
   What time is it?; **Saat ... dir.** It is ...
   o'clock.
saatsaz dükanı watchmaker's
säbäb cause; reason; **bu säbäbdän**
   for that reason
sabah tomorrow; **sabahın(ız) kheyir!**
   good morning!
sabun soap
säbzävätchı greengrocer
sach hair
sach käsmäk haircut
sach qurudan hairdryer
sädr speaker
säfärin mäqsädi reason for travel

säfir ambassador
säfirlik embassy
safsar ferret
sagh ol(un)! thank you!; good by!
sagh alive; right *(side)*
sagh-salamat safe *adjective*
saghchı right-wing
saghlam healthy
saghlamlıq health
saghlıq toast *drink*
saghol! cheers!
sahä field
sähär morning;**bu sähär** this morning
sähär saat . . . a.m.
sähär yemäyi breakfast
sahib host; owner
sahib olmaq own *verb*
sahil coast; shore; river bank
Sähiyyä Nazirliyi Ministry of Health
sähiyyä healthcare
sähnä stage; podium
sähra desert
sähv mistake
sähv etmäk make a mistake
sakhlamaq keep; park; stop **sakhla!**
    stop!; **sakhlama!** don't stop!; **Män
    säfirliyimizlä älaqä sakhlamaq
    istäyiräm.** I want to contact my
    embassy.
sakhta: Bu pul sakhtadır. This
    money is counterfeit.
sakhta pul counterfeit money
sakit *adjective* quiet
sakitjä quietly
sakitläshdiriji tranquilizer
säkkız eight
säksän eighty
salam (äleyküm)! hello!
salat salad
salon salon shop
sallanmaq swing
säma air; sky
samavar samovar
sän *singular* you
sän özün yourself
sänädl document
sänädli film documentary film
sänät business
sänätkar craftsman
sänaye industry
sänin your; yours *singular*
saniyä second *noun*
sanjaq pin; safety pin
sanjmaq sting
sap thread

säpin planting
saqqal beard
saqqız chewing gum
saray palace
särgi exhibition
särgüzäsht adventure
särhäddchi border guard
särhädd kechidi border crossing
särhädd qoshunları border guard
sarı yellow
sarılıq khästäliyi hepatitis
sarıma *medical* sling
sarımsaq garlic
särin cool; fresh
särkhosh drunk
särnishin passenger
sarsagh thick *dense*
säs sound; voice; vote
säs-küy noise
säs-küylü noisy
säs vermä voting
säs vermäk *verb* vote
säs vermänin saxtalashdırılması
    vote-rigging
säs yazma avadanlıghı sound
    equipment
sässiz silent
satıjı salesperson
satmaq sell
säviyyä *noun* level
säya hätchi traveler
säyahät travel *noun*
säyahätä chıkhmaq travel *verb*
saymaq count *verb*
säyyar ev caravan
sazish imzalamaq to sign an
    agreement
sechkilär election
sechmäk choose; elect
seks sex
Sentyabr September
septik septic
sessiya session
sevgi love
sevimli dear; loved
sevmäk like; love
seyf safe box
seysmolozhi tädqiqat seismic survey
seyyidin mäzarı saint's tomb
shäfa vermäk heal
shäfäq dawn
shaftalı peach
shagird pupil
shah shah
shähär city; town

shähär märkäzi city center; town center
shähärätrafı qäsäbä suburb
shähärin khäritäsi city map
shahid witness
shähid martyr
shair poet
shäkär khästäliyi diabetes
shakhmat chess
shäkhs person
shakhta frost; mine; coal mine
shakhtachı miner
shakhtalı freezing
shäkil form; shape; image; picture; painting
shäkilä salmaq *verb* form
shälälä waterfall
shalban plank
shalvar trousers
sham aghajı pine
sham candle
sham yemäyi dinner; supper
shamdan candlestick
shampan champagne
shampun shampoo
Shänbä Saturday
shänlik party
shärf scarf
shärq east
shärqi east; eastern
shey thing; **Bir shey deyil.** It doesn't matter.
sheytan devil
shifoner cupboard
shikäst disabled
shikayät complaint
shikayätlänmäk complain
shimal north *noun*
shimali north; northern
Shimali Írlandiya Northern Ireland
shimshäk lightning
shin splint *(medical)*; tire *(vehicle)*
shirin sweet
shirniyyat candy
shishmäk swell
shivä dialect
shkaf cupboard
shlanq hose
shok shock *medical*
shokolad chocolate
shorba soup
shotka brush
Shotland Scottish
Shotlandiya Scotland
shtab staff
shtat state *(in federation)*

shübhä doubt
shübhäsiz *adverb* sure; no doubt
shumlamaq plow
shura council
shüshä achan bottle opener
shüshä glass; bottle; **bir shüshä chakhır/shäräb** bottle of wine; **bir shüshä pivä** bottle of beer; **bir shüshä su** bottle of water
sichan mouse
sichovul rat
sidi CD
sidi pleyer CD player
sifarish edilib reserved
sifarish etmäk reserve; order a meal; **Män yer sifarish edä bilärämmi?** Can I reserve a place?; **Mänim otaghım sifarish olunub.** I have a reservation.
sifarishli mäktub registered mail
sıfır nought; zero
sıghınajaq shelter
sıghorta insurance; **Mänim tibbi sıghortam vardır.** I have medical insurance.
sıghorta polis; sıghorta sänädi insurance policy
silah weapon
silahlar zibilkhanası arms dump
silsilä series
simfoniya symphony
simptom symptom
simvol symbol
sinä chest
sınaq test *noun*
sinaqoq synagogue
sındırmaq fracture *verb*
sinif class
sınıq fracture *noun*
sınma fracture *noun*
sintaksis syntax
siqara cigar
siqaret(lär) cigarette(s)
siqaret chäkmäk qadaghandır no smoking
siqaret chäkmäk smoking
siqaret kaghızı cigarette papers
sıragha gün the day before yesterday
sırghalar earrings
sirkä vinegar
sirr secret *noun*
sırsıra solstice
sistem system
sitrus citrus

siyahı list
siyasät politics
siyasätchi politician
siyasi partiya party *political*
siyasi political
siz özünüz yourselves
siz you *plural*
-sız/-siz without
sizin your; yours *plural*
sızmaq pour out
söhbät conversation
sol left
solchu left-wing
sol-qanadlı left-wing
son noun end
son zamanlar recently
sona chatdırmaq *verb* end
söndürmäk switch off
sönük pale
sonunju *adjective* final
sonunju last
soraq kitabchası manual *(book)*
sorghu enquiry
sorqu kitabı directory
sorushmaq ask
soruyuju pump *noun*
sosial social
sosialist socialist
sosializm socialism
Sovet İttifaqı Soviet Union
soymaq rob; **Mäni soyublar.** I've been robbed.
soyqırım massacre; genocide
soyuqdäymä *medical* cold
soyuduju fridge
soyuduju refrigerator
soyughdur it is cold
soyuq cold; **soyuq su** cold water
soyuqdäymä flu
soyuqlamaq: Män soyuqlamısham. I have a cold.
söyüsh söymäk swear; curse
sözlük dictionary
spid khästäliyi AIDS
spiker speaker *parliament*
sportsmen athlete
stadion stadium
stäkan glass; **bir stäkan su** glass of water
stansiya station
stetoskop stethoscope
stol table
struktur structure
sü'ni artificial
su water; **su shüshäsi** water bottle

sual question
subay single; **Män subayam.** I am single.
sübut evidence; proof
sübut etmäk prove
süd maghazası dairy
süd milk
südlü chay tea with milk
süfrä tablecloth
sui-qäsd assassination
sükan steering wheel
sükut silence
sülh peace
sülh danıshıqları peace talks
sülhü-qoruyuju qüvvälär peace-keeping troops
sultan sultan
sümük bone
sümük qabarı callus
sun'i khizäk yolu piste
sunkär sponge
sup soup
süpürmäk sweep
sürät copy
sürät chıkharma mashını photocopier
sür'ät speed
sürätini chıkharmaq copy *verb*
sürgün exile
sürmä mascara
sürmäk continue; drive
sürü flock; herd
sürüjü driver
sürüjü väsiqäsi driver's license
sürüklämäk drag
sürüshmäk slip
sustamaq: Män sustamısham. I'm thirsty.
sütlü qähvä coffee with milk
suvenir dükanı souvenir shop
-suz/-süz without
Svan Svan
svetofor traffic lights
sviter sweater

T

tääjjübediji surprising
täässüf: Män täässüf ediräm. I'm sorry.
täbabät medicine
täbiät nature
täbii natural
täbii ehtiyatlar natural resources
täbii fälakät natural disaster

tÄbil drum
tÄdqiqat research
tÄdqiqatchı scientist; researcher
tÄ'fil vermÄk hand over
tÄhlÜkÄ danger
tÄhlÜkÄsizlik safety
tÄhlÜkÄsizlik security
tÄhqiqat investigation
TÄhsil Nazirliyi Ministry of Education
tÄhsil education
tÄjhizat supply *noun*
tÄ'jili express; urgent
tÄjili yardım mashını ambulance
tÄk alone; single; unique
tÄk otaq single room
tÄkÄr wheel; tire
tÄkÄrli oturajaq wheelchair
takhıl seed
takhıl kombaynı combine harvester
tÄkhminÄn approximately
takht-taj throne
takhta wood *(substance)*
tÄkjÄ *adverb* only
tÄkmillÄshdirmÄk improve
tÄkrar etmÄk repeat
taksi taxi
tÄlÄ trap
tÄlÄbÄ student
tÄlÄbÄ shÄhÄrjiyi; tÄlÄbÄ yataqkhanası campus
tÄlÄfat loss of life; victims
tÄlÄffÜz pronunciation
tÄlÄffÜz etmÄk pronounce
tÄlÄ minalar booby traps
tÄlÄsmÄk to be in a hurry; **MÄn tÄlÄsirÄm.** I'm in a hurry.
Talısh Talysh
tam entire; perfect
tamamilÄ all together
tamasha performance; show
tÄ'mir repair *noun*
tÄ'mir etmÄk repair *verb*
tÄmiz *adjective* clean
tÄmizlÄmÄk *verb* clean
tÄmizlik hygiene
tampon tampon
tÄmsil etmÄk represent
tÄmsilchi representative
tÄnbÄl lazy
tanımaq recognize
tanınmısh well-known
tank tank *military*
tÄpÄ hill
tapanja pistol

tapmaq find
tÄqdim etmÄk introduce
taqqıldatmaq knock
tÄqribÄn almost
tÄqsirlÄndirmÄk accuse
tarakan cockroach
tÄrÄvÄz vegetables
tÄrÄvÄz dÜkanı vegetable shop
tÄrbiyÄ education; upbringing
tÄ'rif praise
tarikh date; history
tarikhchi historian
tÄrjÜmÄ translation
tÄrjÜmÄ etmÄk translate
tÄrjÜmÄchi translator; interpreter
tÄrk etmÄk leave; quit
tÄrlÄmÄk sweat
tas *noun* sink
tÄsÄrrÜfat industry
tÄsÄrrufat malları dÜkanı hardware store
tÄsbeh rosary
tÄshÄbbÜs etmÄk undertake
tÄshÄkkÜr edirÄm! thank you!
tÄshÄkkÜr etmÄk thank
tÄshkil etmÄk arrange
tÄshlikat organisation
tÄshrifat etiquette
tÄsvir etmÄk describe
Tat Tat∕Mountain Jew
tÄ'til strike *(from work)*
tÄ'til etmÄk to strike *(from work)*
tÄvÄllÜd date of birth
tÄvÄllÜd sÄnÄndi birth certificate
taya haystack
tÄyyarÄ airplane
tÄyyarÄ pochtu air mail
tÄyyarÄyÄ minik burakhılıshı boarding pass
tÄzÄ new; fresh
tÄzÄ ay new moon
tazyiq pressure
teatr theater
tekhpasport car papers
tekhnika technique
tel string; wire
telefon telephone
telefon-avtomat public phone
telefon danıshıqları mÄrkÄzi telephone center
telefon kodu dialling code
telefon nÖmrÄsi yıghmaq dial
telefon stansiyası telephone station
telefonchu telephone operator
teleks telex

teleqram telegram
teleskop telescope
televiziya stansiyası television station
televizor television set
tenis tennis
näzäriyyä theory
termometr thermometer
test test
tez early; quick; quickly
tez-tez often
tezliklä soon
tibb bajısı nurse
tibbi medical
tibbi sığorta medical insurance
tikanlı mäftil barbed wire
tıkhaj bath-plug; tampon
tikishlär stitches *surgical*
tikmäk build; sew
tilov ipi string
tin corner
tinbashı crossroads
tip type
tırtıl caterpillar
titrätmäk; titrämäk shake
tokhum etmäk sow
tokhum grain; seed
tökmäk pour; spill
top ball; cannon
topuq ankle
tor net
tormoz brake
torpaq earth
torpaq sahäsini tämizlämäk to clear land
torpaq sürüshmäsi landslide
tost toast *(bread)*
toyuq chicken; hen
toz powder; detergent
traktor tractor
transformator transformer
troleybus trolley bus
tromboz thrombosis
tualet toilet(s)
tualet kaghızı toilet paper
tübik tube
tufan thunderstorm
tüfäng gun; rifle
tuflı shoes
tullamaq throw
tünd dark *of colour*
tunel tunnel
tüpürmäk spit
turist tourist
turist agentliyi travel agent

turist idaräsi tourist office
turist kitabchası guidebook
turist gäzintisi camping
turizm tourism
Türk Turk; Turkish
Türkjä Turkish *(language)*
Türkiyä Turkey
turniket tourniquet
tursh sour
tüstülämäk smoke *verb*
tutma epilepsy
tutmaq hold; catch; contain
tutumaq to catch; **Män oruj tuturam.** I am fasting.
tütün tobacco

U

uca high
üch three; **üch däfä** three times
üchdäbir one-third
üchdäiki two-thirds
uchmaq fly *verb*
üchünjü third *adjective*
uchush flight *plane*
uchushlar departures
uchush nömrä . . . flight number . . .
udmaq swallow; win; **Kim uddu?** Who won?
üfüq horizon
üfürmäk blow
ughur success
ughur(lu) olsun! good luck!
uja tall
ujadan loudly
ujuz cheap
Ukrayna Ukraine
ukrayna dilindä Ukrainian (language)
ulduz star
ulubaba ancestor
ümumi general *adjective*
uniforma uniform
univermaq department store; supermarket
universitet university
untsiya ounce
unutmaq forget
ünvan address
üräk heart
üräk khästäliyi heart condition
üräk tutması heart attack
ürk overcoat
ushaq baby; child
ushaq hakimi pediatrician
ushaqlar children

ushaqlıq womb
ustad craftsman
üstälik in addition to
üstün tutmaq prefer
üstünä onto
üsyanchı rebel *noun*
utandırılmısh ashamed
ütü iron *for clothes*
uydurma lie *noun*
uyghun suitable
uyushduruju maddä drug *narcotic*
üyütmäk grind
üz face
üzän floating
uzanmaq lie down
uzaq distant; far
üzbäüz opposite
üzmä swimming
üzmäk swim
üzqırkhma jihazı razor
üzqırkhma kremi shaving cream
üzqırkhma ülgüjü razorblade
üzr apology
üzr istäyiräm *formal* Sorry!
üzr istäyiräm! excuse me!
üzük ring
üzüm grape
uzun long
uzunluq lengthen
üzv member

V

vä and; **vä ya** or
väba cholera
vadi valley
vähshi wild
vajib significant; **bu vajib deyil** it doesn't matter
vajiblik importance
vakht time
vakhtında on time
val LP
valideynlär parents
valyuta currency
vaqon-restoran dining car
vätän homeland
vätändash citizen
vätändash müharibäsi civil war
vätändash hüquqları civil rights
vätändash müharibäsi civil war
vätändashlıq citizenship
vä ya or
vaza vase
väziyyät position; situation

vedrä bucket
velosiped bicycle
Vels Wales
Velsli Welsh
vena vein
ventilyator fan
vergi qoymaq *verb* tax
vergi *noun* tax
vergidän azad ärazi tax-free zone
verilmäk transmit
vermäk give
vertolyot helicopter
veto veto
videokaset videotape cassette
videomaqnitofon; videopleyer video player
vint screw
vintburan screwdriver
virus virus
vishka derrick
viski whisky
vitse-prezident vice-president
viza visa
vurghu accent
vurmaq beat; hit
vurushma battle

Y

-yä/-ä into
yaba spade
yadda sakhlamaq remember
yaddash memory
yagh bankası oilcan
yagh fat; cooking oil
yaghısh rain
yaghısh yaghır it is raining
yaghlı *adjective* fat
yaghmurlu hava rainy weather
Yahudi dini Judaism
Yähudi Jew; Jewish
yakhın near
yakhında yerläshän nearby
yakhshı good; nice; well
yakhud or
yalan false; lie
yamaj slope
yan küchä sidestreet
yanajaq anbarı fuel dump
yanajaq fuel
yandırmaq burn; light; switch on
yanghın fire
yanında by
yanvar January
yapıshdırmaq stick

Yaponiya Japan
Yaponja Japanese *(language)*
Yaponlı Japanese
yara injury; wound; ulcer
yaralamaq *verb* wound
yaralı injured
yararlı sufficient
yaratmaq create
yardım aid; relief aid
yarghan ravine
yarı half
yarısh competition
yarmaq split
yarpaq leaf
yash age; wet; **Nechä yashın(ız) var?** How old are you?; **Mänim . . . yashım var.** I am . . . years old.
yasha! cheers!
yashamaq dwell; live
yashayısh accommodation
yashayısh evi apartment block
yashıl green
yataq bed
yataq otaghı bedroom
yataq vaqonu sleeping car
yataqkhana hostel
yataqlı torba sleeping bag
yatmagha getmäk to go to bed
yatmaq sleep *verb*
yavash slow
yavashja slowly
yay summer; spring *(metal)*
yayın ortası midsummer
yaymaq spread
yaz spring *(season)*
yazı writing; inscription; record
yazıchı writer
yazmaq write
yeddi seven
yeganä only *adjective*
yelläyän fan
yelläyänin kämäri fan belt
yemäk food; meal; to eat; to consume
yemäk otaghı dining room
yemäk stansiyası feeding station
yemäklär meals
yemish melon
yenä again
Yeni İl Bayramı New Year *(January 1)*
Yeni Zelandiya New Zealand
yeni new
yepiskop bishop
yer ground; land; location; place; seat *(in assembly)*; space

yeraltı kechid subway/underground/ metro
Yerevan Yerevan
yerinä instead
yerinä qoymaq replace
yerli local
yeshik box
yetim orphan
yetishmish ripe
yetmish seventy
yıghınjaq forum; assembly
yırtmaq *verb* tear
yokh no; not
yokhlama mäntäqäsi checkpoint
yokhlama examination; test
yokhlamaq examine; test; check
yokhsul poor
yol atlası road map
yol göstärmäk guide *verb*
yol khäritäsi road map
yol polisi traffic police
yol postu roadblock
yol road; route; track; way; **dagh yolu** mountain pass
yol yoldashı companion
yoldash comrade
yolun(uz) yüngül olsun! bon voyage!
yorghan blanket; quilt
yorghun tired
yorulmaq to tire
yük baggage; cargo; freight
yük yeri boot
yukharı up
yukhu sleep; dream
yukhu därmanı sleeping pill(s)
yukhulu sleepy; **Män yukhuluyam.** I am sleepy.
yüksäk high
yüksäk qan täzyiqi high blood pressure
yumaq wash
yumor humor
yumoristik humorous
yumshaq soft
yumshaq hava thaw
yumshaq qısh mild winter
yumurta egg
yun wool
yun köynäk sweater
Yunan Greek
Yunanja Greek *(language)*
Yunesko UNESCO
yüngül easy; light *(not heavy)*
yurd homeland

yurdsuz homeless
yuyulajaq paltar laundry
yüz hundred
yüzillik century

Z

zabit *military* officer
zäbt etmäk seize
zädälämäk injure
zagha cave
zähär poison
zäif weak
zälzälä earthquake
zaman time; period
zäng bell
zäng etmäk phone; ring
zängin rich
zänjir chain
zänn etmäk think
zännimjä ... I think ...

zarafat etmäk fool *verb*
zarafat joke
zärär injury; harm
zärärli harmful
zärb-mäsäl proverb
zärf envelope
zärgärlik malları jewelry
zheton token *coin*
zhurnal magazine
zhurnalist journalist
zibil garbage
zirehli mashın armored car
zirvä summit; top; peak
zirvä görüshü summit conference
ziyarätchı pilgrim
zöhrävi khastälik venereal disease
zona area
zoopark zoo
zorakılıq violence
zorlama rape; **Mäni zorlayıblar.** I've been raped.

ENGLISH-AZERBAIJANI
İNGİLİSJÄ-AZÄRBAYJANJA

A

ability qabiliyyät
Abkhaz abkhaz
Abkhazia Abkhazya
able: to be able bajarmaq
about baräsindä
academic elmi ishchi
academy akademiya; **academy of sciences** Elmlär Akademiyasi
accelerator qaz pedalı
accent vurghu
access: Do you have access for the disabled? Sizdä älillär üchün girish varmı?
accident avariya; **There's been an accident.** Órada yol-näqliyyat hadisäsi bash verib.
accommodation mäskän; yashayısh
according to . . . görä; . . . äsasän
accountant muhasib
accuse taqsırlandırmaq; *legal* ittiham etmäk
activist fäal
actor aktyor
actual häqiqi
adapter adapter
add artırmaq; älavä etmäk
addition: in addition to üstälik
address únvan
administrator administrator
admiral admiral
adventure mäjara; särgüzäsht; *story* ähvalat
afraid: to be afraid of qorkhmaq
after dalında
afternoon günortadan sonra; **good afternoon!** Gunortan(ız)* kheyir!; **this afternoon** bu gün
afterwards nätijädä
again yenä
age yash
ago bundan ävväl
agreement razılıq; **to sign an agreement** sazish imzalamaq
agriculture känd täsärrufatı
agronomist aqronom
aid yardım; **humanitarian aid** humanitar yardım; **first aid** ilk yardım

aid worker humanitar yardım ishchisi
AIDS eyds khästäliyi; spid khästäliyi
air hava, säma
air-conditioner; air-conditioning kondisioner
airforce härbi hava donanması; hava qüvväläri
airline hava yolları shirkäti
air mail aviapocht, täyyarä pochtu
airplane täyyarä
airport aeroport; hava limanı
airport tax aeroport vergisi
air raid hava hüjumu
alcohol alkohol
alcoholic ichki düshkünü; äyyash
alcoholism äyyashlıq
alive diri; saghı
all bütün; här
all together tamamilä
allergic: I'm allergic to . . . Mänim . . . qarshı allergiyam var.
allergy allergiya
allow ijazä vermäk
almost täqribän
alone täk
alphabet älifba
already artıq; daha
also bundan bashqa, hämchinin
alter däyishmäk
although härchänd
always hämishä; daim
a.m. sähär saat . . .
ambassador säfir
ambulance täjili yardım mashını
ambush *noun* hämlä; pusqu
America Amerika
American amerikalı
among ortasında
amount kämiyyät
amputation amputasiya
analysis analiz
ancestor ulubaba
ancient qädim
and vä; **both . . . and** här . . . ikisi
anemia qan chatıshmazlıqı
anesthetic keyläshdiriji
anesthetist anesteziyachı
angle bujaq
angry äsäbli

animal heyvan
ankle topuq
annoyed: I am annoyed ajıqlandırılmısh
another daha bir
answer javab
ant qarıshka
anti-freeze antifriz
anti-personnel mine piyadalara qarshi mina
anti-vehicle mine mashınlara qarshı mina
antibiotic antibiotik
antibiotics antibiotiklär
antiseptic antiseptik
anyone här käs; här birisi
anywhere bir yerdä
apartment mänzil
apartment block yashayısh evi
apologize: I apologize. Män sizdän üzr istäyiräm.
apology üzr
appear görünmäk
appendicitis appendisit
apple alma
appliances jihaz
approximately täkhminän
April Aprel
Arab äräb
Arabic *language* äräbjä
archeological arkheolozhi
archeology arkheologiya
architect me'mar
architecture me'marlıq
area ärazi
area code ärazi kodu (indeksi)
arm äl
Armenia Ermänistan
Armenian ermäni; *language* ermänijä
armored car zirehli mashın
arms dump silahlar zibilkhanası
army ordu
arrange täshkil etmäk
arrest häbs etmäk
arrivals gälish
arrive gälmäk
art injäsänät
art gallery injäsänät qalereyası
artery äsas qan damarı
article mäqalä
artificial sü'ni
artificial limb protez
artillery artileriya
artist rässam
as kimi
as much onun qädarındä
ashamed utandırılmısh

ashtray külgabı
ask sorushmaq
aspirin aspirin
assassin qatil
assassination sui-qäsd
assembly yıghınjaq; mäjlis
asthma astma
asthmatic astmalı
at least än azı
athlete sportsmen; idmanchı
athletics atletika
atlas atlas
attack *noun* hämlä
attack *verb* hämlä etmäk
August avqust
Australia Avstraliya
Australian avstraliyalı
author avtor
auto supply shop ehtiyat hissäläri maghazası
autonomous mukhtar
autonomy özünü-idarä; mukhtariyyat
autumn payız
avalanche qar uchqunu; chıgh
Avar Avar
average *adjective* orta; normal
awake ayıq
axe balta
Azerbaijan Azärbayjan
Azeri, Azerbaijani Azärbayjanlı; *language* Azärbayjanja

B

B&W (film) agh-qara plyonka
baby ushaq
back *adverb* arkha
back *noun* bel
backache bel aghrısı
backpack baghlama
backwards geriyä
bacteria bakteriya
bad pis
badly pis
bag chanta
baggage baqazh; yük; **excess baggage** artıq baqazh
baggage counter baqazh bölmäsi
bake bishirmäk
baker's chöräk maghazası
bakery chöräkkhana
Baku Bakı
balcony balkon; eyvan
Balkar balkar
ball top
ballet balet
ballpoint diyirjäkli qäläm
Band-Aid plastır

bandit quldur
bank bank; **river bank** sahil
banker bank ishchisi; maliyyächi
bank notes kaghız pulu
banquet banket
bar bar
barbed wire tikanlı mäftil
barber's bärbärkhana; dälläkkhana
bark *verb* hürmäk
barley arpa
barn päyä
barracks barak
barrel bochka; chälläk
barren barsız
bartender barmen
base baza
basement podval
basin hövzä
basis bazis
basket kuzov
basketball basketbol
bathe chimmäk
bathroom hamam otaghı
battery batareya; *car* akumulyator
battle vurushma
bay körfäz
be olmaq
beach plyazh; chimärlik
beans pakhla; lobya
bear ayı
beard saqqal
beat vurmaq
beautiful gözäl
beauty gözällik
beauty parlor kosmetika kabinäsı
because chünki
because of ona görä
become olmaq
bed yataq; **to go to bed** yatmagha
    gätmäk
bedroom yataq otaghı
bee arı
beef mal äti
beer pivä
beetroot chughundur
before irälidä
begin bashlamaq
beginning ävväli
behind arkhada
believe inanmaq
bell zäng
below ashaghı
belt kämär
bend *in road* döngä
bend *verb* äymäk
berry gilämeyvä
besides bundan bashqa

best än yakhshı
betray khäyanät etmäk
better daha yakhshı
better: I feel better. Män özümü
    daha yakhshı hiss ediräm.
between arasında
Bible Bibliya; İnjälik
bicycle velosiped
big böyük
biggest daha böyük
bill hesab
binoculars durbin
biography bioqrafiya
bird qush
birth anadan olma; doghum; **to give
    birth to** doghmaq
birth certificate tävällüd sänändi
birth control hamiläliyin qashısını
    alan tädbirlär
birthday anadan olma günü
bishop yepiskop
bit: little bit bir az
bite dishlämäk
bitter ajı
black qara
black market qara bazar
blanket yorghan
bleed qan akhmaq
blind kor
blizzard qarlı boran
blocked: The toilet is blocked.
    Tualetin borusu tutulub.
blood qan
blood group qan qrupu
blood pressure qan täzyiqi
blood transfusion qan köchürülmäsi
blow üfürmäk
blow up partlatmaq
blue qöy
blues blyuz
board council idarä
boarding pass täyyaräyä kechid
    burakhılıshı; minik väräqäsi
boat gämi
body bädän
boil *noun* qaynar su
boil *verb* qaynamaq
bomb bomba
bomb disposal bombaları
    zärärsizläshdirmä
bombardment bombardman
bomber bombardman täyyarä
bon appetit! Nush olsun!
bon voyage! Yolun(uz)* yüngül olsun!
bone sümük
bonnet *of car* kapot
booby trap(s) tälä mina(lar)

book

book kitab
bookshop kitab maghazası
boot baqazh yeri; yük yeri; *of car*
boots chākmālār
border hüdud
border crossing sārhādd kechidi
border guard sārhādchi
born: I was born in . . . Mān . . .
anadan olmusham.
born: Where were you born? Siz
harada anadan olmusuz?
borrow borj almaq
boss boss
both hār iki(si)
both . . . and onu da . . . bunu da
bottle shūshā; **bottle of beer** bir
shūshā pivā; **bottle of water** bir
shūshā su; **bottle of wine** bir
shūshā chakhır/shārāb
bottle opener shūshā achan
bottom arkha; dal; dib
box yeshik
boxing boks
boy oghlan
boyfriend oghlan dostu
bracelet qolbagh
brake tormoz
brandy brendi; konyak
brave jāsur
bread chörāk
break for refreshments qısa
qalyanaltıfasiläsi
break *verb* qırmaq
**break down: Our car has broken
down.** Bizim mashınımız sınıb.
breakfast sāhār yemāyi
breast chest sinā
breath nāfās
breed *verb* böyütmāk
brick kārpich
bridge körpü
bring gātirmāk
Britain Britaniya
British Britaniyalı
brooch brosh
brother qardash
brown qāhvāyi
bruise göy; qanchır
brush fırcha, shotka
bucket vedrā
Buddhism Budda dini
Buddhist buddist; budda dindarı
budget būjā
build tıkmāk
building bina
bull gamısh
bullet güllā

bumper bamper
bureaucracy bürokratism
burn yandırmaq
burst partlamaq
bury basdırmaq
bus avtobus
bus station avtovaghzal
bus stop avtobus dayanajaghı
business ishkūzar sāfār; biznes;
enterprise sānāt
business class biznes klass
businessman/woman ishkūzar adam;
biznesmen
busy: The line is busy. O,
māshquldur.
but lakin
butane canister qaz balonu
butcher's āt dūkanı
butterfly kāpānāk
buy almaq
by yanında

C

cabbage (bash) kālām
cabinet kabinet
cable māftil; kabel; khātt
calculator kalkulyator
calf *cow* buzor
call zāng vurmaqı chaghırmaq; **Call
the police.** Polisi chagır.
called: What're you called? Sizin
adınız nādir? **I'm called Fred.**
Mānim adım Freddir.
callus sūmūk qabarı
camel dāvā; hār
camera fotoaparat; kamera
camera equipment fotokamera
avadanlıghı
camp: Can we camp here? Burada
dūshārgā qurmaq olarmı?
camping kemping; turist qāzintisi
campsite dūshārgā yeri
campus kampus; tālābā yataqkhanası;
tālābā shāhārjiyi
can *noun* banka
can *verb: see* **able**
can opener konserva achan
Canada Kanada
Canadian Kanadalı
canal kanal
cancel lāghv etmāk
cancelled: The plane is cancelled.
cancer khārchāng
candle sham
candlestick shamdan
candy shirniyyat
canister kanistra

cannon top
capital *financial* kapital; maliyya
capital city paytakht
capsicum bibär
car mashın; avtomobil
car papers mashının sänädläri; tekh pasport
car park avtomobil dayanajaqı
car registration qeydiyyat nömräsi
car supply store ehtiyat hissäläri maghazası
caravan kärvan; säyyar ev
care qayghı; qayghısına qalmaq
careful ehtiyatlı
cargo yük
carpenter kharrat
carpet khalcha
carrier bag chanta
carry aparmaq
cart araba
carton of cigarettes bir qutu siqaret
cashier kassir
cashier's booth kassa
casino kazino; qumarkhana
Caspian Sea Khäzär Dänizi
cassette kaset
castle qala
cat pishik
catch tutmaq
caterpillar tırtıl
cathedral kirkha
Catholic katolik
cattle iri buynuzlu heyvanlar
Caucasus Qafqaz
Caucasus Mountains Qafqaz Daghları
cause säbäb
cave maghara, kaha, zagha
caviar kürü
CD sidi; kompakt disk
CD player sidi pleyer
ceasefire atäshkäs
cellar podval
cemetery qäbiristanlıq
center märkäz
century yüzillik
ceramics keramika
certain müäyyän
certainly älbättä; däqiq
chain zänjir
chair kreslo; kürsü; oturajaq
champagne shampan
change: I want to change some dollars. Män bir az dollar däyishmäk istäyiräm.
channel kanal
chapter fäsil; hissä

character kharakter; **in book etc** *qähräman*
charge haqq; mäsuliyyät; **What is the charge?** Nä qädär vermäliyäm?; **Who is in charge?** Buranın böyüyü kimdir?
charity *organization* kheyriyyächilik
chase ovlamaq; dalınja düshmäk
cheap ujuz
cheaper daha ujuz
Chechen chechen
Chechnya Chechenistan
check *money* chek
check *verb*: **Could you please check that again?** Zähmät olmasa, bunu bir dä yokhlayın?; **Check the oil please.** Zähmät olmasa, yaghı yokhlayın.
check-in qeydiyyat
check-in counter qeydiyyat bölmäsi
checkpoint yokhlama mäntäqäsi
cheers! yashal; saghol!!
cheese pendir
chemical kimyävi
chemistry kimyä
chess shakhmat
chest sinä
chew cheynämäk
chewing gum saqqız
chicken toyuq
chief bashchı
child ushaq
children ushaghlar
chimney dudkesh
chin chänä
Chinese Chin dilindä
chocolate shokolad
choir khor
choke boghulmaq; **He is choking.** Onun boghazında nä isä galıb!
cholera väba
choose sechmäk
chop käsmäk
Christian *adjective* khristian
Christian *noun* khachpäräst
Christianity khristianlıq; khachpärästlik
Christmas Milad Bayramı
church kilsä
cigar siqara
cigarette papers siqaret kaghızı
cigarette(s) siqaret(lär)
cinema kinoteatr
Circassian chärkäs
circle dairä
citizenship vätändashlıq
citizen vätändash

citrus sitrus
city shähär
city center shähär märkäzi
city hall ratusha
city map shähärin khäritäsi
civil rights vätändash hüquqları
civil war vätändash müharibäsi
civilian mülki adam
class sinif
classical music klassik musiqi
clean *adjective* tämiz; clean sheets tämiz mäläfä
clean *verb* tämizlämäk
clear *adjective* aydın
clear land torpagh sahäsini tämizlämäk
clear mines minanı zärärsizläshdirmäk
climate mühit
clinic klinika; khästäkhana
clock saat
close baghlamaq; What time does it close? Bu nä zaman baghlanır?
closed baghlı
clothes paltar
clothes shop paltar dükanı
cloud bulud
cloudy buludlu
clown kloun
club klub
clutch *of car* qoshqu
coal kömür
coal mine shakhta; kömür mä'däni
coast sahil
coat palto
cockroach tarakan; mätbäkhböjäyi
code kod; international code beynälkhalq kod
coffee qähvä; coffee with milk sütlü qähvä
cognac konyak
coins dämir pulu
cold *adjective* soyuq; cold water soyuq su; it is cold soyughdur; I am cold. Mänä soyuqdur.
cold *noun medical* soyuqdäymä; I have a cold. Män soyuqlamısham.
colleague hämkar
collective farm kolkhoz
college kollej
color räng
color film rängli plyonka
colorless rängsiz
comb daragh
combine harvester takhıl kombaynı
come gälmäk
come in! gälin ichäri!

comfortable rahat
commission komissiya faizi
commission: What is the commission? Komissiya faizi nä qädärdir?
communications komunikasiyalar; rabitä
communism komunizm
Communist komunist
community ijma
companion yol yoldashı
compare müqayisä etmäk
compass kompas
compensation kompensasiya; qarshılıq
competition müsabiqä; yarısh
complain shikayätlänmäk
complaint shikayät
composer kompozitor
composition insha
computer kompyuter; bilgisayar
comrade yoldash
concentration camp konslaqer, häbs düshärgäsi
concert konsert
concert hall konsert zalı
concert konsert
concussion *medical* beyin sarsıntısı
condition hal
condom prezervativ; goruyuju
conference konfrans
conference room konfrans otaghı
confuse qarıshıq salmaq
connection älaqä
conquer istila etmäk
constipation qäbälik
constitution konstitusiya; äsas qanun
consulate konsulluq
consultant mäslähätchi
consume yemäk
contact lenses kontakt linzaları
contact lens solution kontakt linzaları üchün tämizläyiji
contact: I want to contact my embassy. Män säfirliyimizlä älaqä sakhlamaq istäyiräm.
contain tutmaq
container *freight* konteyner
contemporary müasir
contest konkurs
continue sürmäk
contract kontrakt
control kontrol
conversation danıshıq; söhbät
convoy konvoy; müshayyät
cook *noun* ashpaz
cook *verb* bishirmäk

cooker mätbäkh sobası
cool särin
cooperation ämäkdashlıq
copper mis
copse jäsäd; meyit
copy noun sürät
copy verb sürätini chıkharmaq
cork stopper mantar
corkscrew burghu; probkaachan
corn qarghudalı
corner tin
correct adjective düzgün
correct verb düzältmäk
corruption rüshvätkhorluq
cost qiymät; **How much does this cost?** Bunu qiymäti nä qädärdir?
cotton pambıgh
cotton wool pambıgh
cough ösküräk
council shura
count verb saymaq
counterfeit sakhta pul; **This money is counterfeit.** Bu pul sakhtadır.
country ölkä; **in the country** känd yeri
countryside
coup d'état dövlät chevrilishi
courier kuriyer
court law mähkämä
cow inäk
craftsman ustad; sänätkar
crane machine kran
crash avariya
crazy däli
create yaratmaq
credit kredit
credit card kredit kartı
crime jinayät
criminal jinayätkar
crisis böhran
crops äkin sahäläri
cross verb käsishmäk
crossing käsishmä; kechid
crossroads tinbashi; dörd yol aghzi
crow bird qargha
crude oil kham neft
cruel rähmsiz
cry chıghırmaq
crystal büllur; kristal
cucumber khiyar
culture mädäniyyät
cup fincan
cupboard dolab, shkaf, shifoner
cure noun müalijä
cure verb müalijä etmäk
currency pul; valyuta
custom tradition adät

customs border gömrük
cut verb käsmäk; **The lines have been cut.** Khättlär käsilib.
cutoff: I've been cut off. Söhbätimi käsdilär.; **The electricity has been cut off.** Ishiq käsilib.; **The gas has been cut off.** Qaz käsilib.; **The heating has been cut off.** Isitmä käsilib.; **The water has been cut off.** Su käsilib.

D

dagger khänjär
Daghestan Daghıstan
Daghestani daghıstanlı
dairy süd maghazası
dam damba
dance; dancing räqs
danger tählükä
Danish danimarka dilindä
dark adjective tänd
dark; darkness noun qaranlıq
date tarikh; fruit tin; **What date is it today?** Bu gün hansi gündür?
date of arrival gälish tarikhi
date of birth tävällüd; anadan olan gün
date of departure gedish tarikhi
daughter qız
dawn noun shäfäq
day gün
daytime gündüz
dead ölü
deaf kar
dear loved sevimli
death ölüm
debt borj
decade onillik
December dekabr
decide qärara gälmäk
decision qärar
deep därin
deep water platform därin sular üchün platforma
deer maral
defeat mäghlubiyyät
defend müdafiä etmäk
delay gejikmä
delayed: The plane is delayed. Täyyarä gejikir.
democracy demokratiya
democratic demokratik
demonstration political nümayish
demonstrators political nümayishchilär
dentist dish häkimi
deodorant deodorant
department store univermaq

departures uchushlar; gedishlär
deport kharij etmäk
deportation kharij etmä;
   deportasiya
depot depo
deprive m|ahrum etmäk
derivative noun derivativ
derrick vyshka; buruq
describe täsvir etmäk
desert noun sähra
desert verb boshaltmaq
desire verb arzulamaq
desk masa
dessert desert
destroy daghıtmaq
detergent toz
development inkishaf
devil sheytan
diabetes diabet; shäkär khästäliyi
diabetic diabet khästäsi
diagnosis diaqnoz
dial telefon nömräsi yığhmaq
dialect shivä; lähchä
dialling code telefon kodu
diarrhea ishal
dictator diktator
dictatorship diktatorluq
dictionary sözlük
die ölmäk
diesel dizel
diet diyeta
different färqli
difficult chätin
dig qazımaq
digital räqämli
dine nahar etmäk
dining car vaqon-restoran
dining room yemäk otaghı
dinner sham yemäyi
diplomat diplomat
diplomatic ties diplomatik älaqälär
direct birbasha; därhal; **Can I dial
   direct?** Män birbasha nömräni
   yığha bilärämmi?
directions istiqamätlär
directory sorqu kitabı
dirty chirkin; chirkli
disabled älil; shikäst
disaster fajiä; **natural disaster** täbii
   fälakät
disco disko
discover käshf etmäk
discuss müzakirä etmäk
discussion müzakirä
disease khästälik
disk jockey disk zhokey
Displaced Person mäjburi köchkün

dispute mübahisä
dissolve ärimäk
distant uzaq
district rayon; ärazi
diver dalghıj
divide bölmäk
divorced boshanmısh **I am divorced.**
   Män boshanmısham.
dizzy: I feel dizzy. Bashım gijälänir.
do not . . . ! . . . etmäk!
do etmäk; **What do you do?** Siz nä
   ilä mäshqulsunuz?
doctor häkim
dock liman
document sänäd
documentary film sänädli film
dog it
doll kukla; gälinjik
dollar dolar
donkey eshshäk
door qapı
doorlock kilid
double iki däfä artıq; **double bed** ikiliy
   yataq; **double room** ikinäfärlik otaq
doubt shübhä
down ashaghı
drag sürüklämäk
drain drenazh
draw dartmaq
drawer räf
dream noun yukhu
dress noun paltar; don
dressed: to get dressed geyinmäk
dressmaker paltarkäsän; därzi
drill noun qazıma mashını
drill a well quyu qazımaq
drilling qazıma
drink noun ichki
drink verb ichmäk
drinking water ichmäli su
drive sürmäk
driver sürüjü
driver's license sürüjü väsiqäsi
drug därman; narcotic uyushduruju
   maddä
drug addict narkoman
drum täbil
drunk särkhosh
duck ördäk
during müddätindä
Dutch person hollandiyalı; thing
   holland
duty: customs duty gömrük
dwell yashamaq
dynamo dinamo

E

each här
each other här biri
eagle qartal
ear qulaq
early tez
earrings sırghalar
earth torpagh
earthquake zälzälä
east *noun* shärq
east(ern) *adjective* shärqi
easy yüngül
eat yemäk
economics iqtisadiyyat
economist iqtisadchı
economy *saving* qänaät; *of country* täsärrüfat
editor redaktor
education tärbiyä
egg yumurta
eight säkkız
eighteen on säkkız
eighty säksän
elbow dirsäk
elder *noun* aghsakkal
elect sechmäk
election sechkilär
electrical goods store elektrik jihazlar maghazası
electricity ishıq; elektrik
elevator lift
eleven on bir
e-mail elektron pochtu
e-mail address elektron pochtu ünvanı
embassy säfirlik
emergency avariya
emergency exit avariya chıkhıshı
empty *adjective* bosh
empty *verb* boshaltmaq
enamel mina
end *noun* son
end *verb* sona chatdırmaq
enemy düshmän
engine mühärrik
engineer mühändis
England Ingiltärä
English *people/things* Ingilis
English *language* Ingilisjä
enough kifayätdir; **That's enough, thanks.** Kifayätdir, sagh olun.
enquiry sorghu
enter girmäk
enterprise müässis
entire tam
entrance girish
envelope zärf

epidemic epidemiya
epilepsy tutma; epilepsiya
epileptic epilepsiyalı
equipment avadanlıq
-er/-est daha . . .
era era
eraser pozan
escalator eskalator
escape qachmaq
especially khüsusilä
essay insha
establish qurmaq
ethnic cleansing milli (etnik) tämizlämä
etiquette davranısh; etiket; täshrifat
euro *currency* yuro
Europe Avropa
European *adjective* Avropalı
European Union Avropa Ittifaqı
evening akhsham
evening: good evening! Akhshamın(ız)* kheyır!
every här
everybody; everyone här käs
every day här gün
everything härshäy
evidence sübut
exact däqiq
exam imtahan
examine yokhlamaq
example nümunä
excellent ä'la
except (for) . . . bashqa
excess baggage artıgh baqazh
exchange däyishmä
exchange rate: What's the exchange rate? Däyishmä dayarı nä qädärdir?
excluded kharij olaraq; kharij edilmish
excuse *noun* baghıshlama
excuse me! Üzr istäyiräm!; Baghıshlayın!
execute ijra etmäk
execution e'dam
executioner jällad
exercise mäshq
exhaust *of car* ishlänmish qazın chıkhması üchün boru
exhibit *verb* hümayish etmäk
exhibition särgi
exile sürgün
exit chıkhısh
expect gözlämäk
expel qovmaq
expensive baha
explain izah etmäk
explanation izahat
explode partlamaq

exploration akhtarısh
explosion partlayısh
explosives partlayıjı maddä
export *noun* ikhrajat
export *verb* ikhraj etmäk
express *fast* ekspress; tä'jili
express *verb* ifadä etmäk
extend genishländirmäk
extra älavä; **an extra blanket** älavä yorghan
eye göz
eyeglasses gözlük
eyesight mänzärä

F

face üz
fact häqiqät; fäkt
factory fabrika; müässisä
failure mäghlubiyyät
fall *autumn* payız
fall *verb* düshmäk
fallowland herik sahä
false yalan
family ailä
famous mäshhur
fan ventilyator; yelläyän
fan belt yelläyänin kämäri
far uzaq; **How far is the next village?** Növbäti känd nä qädär uzaqdır?
fare: **What is the fare?** Bunun qiymäti nä qädärdir?
farm ferma
farmer fermer; kändli;
farming ferma täsärrufatchılıghı
Farsi farscha
fashion *clothes* moda
fashion däb
fast *quick* jäld
fasting: **I am fasting.** Män oruj tuturam.
fat *adjective* yaghlı; **to get fat** kökälmäk
fat *noun* yagh
father ata
faucet kran
fax faks
fax machine faks mashını
fear *noun* qorkhu
fear *verb* qorkhmaq
February fevral
federation federasiya
feeding station yemäk stansiyası
feel hiss etmäk
feeling hissiyyat
female *adjective* ärdä
female *noun* qadın
fence chäpär
fender bamper

ferret safsar
ferry bärä
fertile bähräli
fertilizer peyin
feud düshmänchilik
fever qızdırma
field sahä
fifteen on besh
fifty älli
fight döyüshmäk
fighter döyüshchü
file *paper* qovluq; *computer* fayl
fill doldurmaq
fill in form formanı doldurmaq
film *movie* film; *for camera* plyonka
filmmaker kino sänätkarı
filtered filtrli
filterless filtrsiz
final *adjective* sonunju
final *noun* final
finance finans; maliyyä
find tapmaq
find out ashkar etmäk
fine *adjective* gözäl
fine *adverb* chokh gözäl
fine *of money* pul järimäsi
finger barmaq
finish *verb* qurtarmaq
fire yanghın
firewood odun, chör-chöp
first birinji
first class birinji klas
fish balıq
fishing balıq ovu
five besh
fix bärkitmäk
flash flash
flashlight fänär; prozhektor
flea bit
fleas bitlär
flee qachmaq
flight *plane* uchush
flight number ... uchush nömrä ...
flint müshtük
floating üzän
flock sürü; nakhır
flood dashqın
floor *ground* döshämä; *storey* qat
florist gül dükanı
flour khämir
flower gül
flu qrip; soyuqdäymä
flush: **The toilet won't flush.** Tualet ishlämir.
fly *noun* qara milchäk
fly *verb* uchmaq
fog duman

foggy dumanlı
folk *noun* jamaat
folk *adjective* khalq
folk dancing khalq rāqsi
folklore folklor
folk music khalq musiqisi
food yemāk
fool *noun* akhmaq
fool *verb* zarafat etmāk
foot ayaq; *measurement* fut
football futbol
foothills dagh ātāyi
footpath jıghır
forbid qadaghan etmāk
forbidden qadaghan edilmish
foreign khariji
foreigner ājnābi
forest meshā
forget unutmaq
fork chāngāl
form *noun* forma; shākil; *official* anket; blank
form *verb* shākilā salmaq
fort qala
fortnight iki hāftā
forty qırkh
forum forum; yıghınjaq; mājlis
forward *adjective* qabaq
forward *verb* irālilāmāk
forwards irāliyā
found *verb* āsası qoymaq
foundation *organization* fond
four dörd
four-wheel drive jip
fourteen on dörd
fourth dördünjü
fracture *noun* sınıq; sınma
fracture *verb* sındırmaq
franc frank
free azad; **Is this seat free?** Bu oturajaq boshdurmu?
free of charge pulsuz
freedom azadlıq
freeze donmaq
freezing shakhtalı; bārk soyuq
freight *noun* freyt; yük
freight *verb* dashımaq
French *person* Fransız
French *language* Fransızja
french fries qızardılmısh kartof
fresh tāzā
fresh *cool* sārin
Friday jümā
fridge soyuduju
friend dost
frighten qorkhutmaq
frog qurbagha

front *noun* qabagh; **in front of** qabaghında
frontier hüdud
frost shakhta
frostbite donma
frostbitten hands/feet dondurulmush āllār/ayaqlar
fruit meyvā
fruit juice meyvā suyu
fuel yanajaq
fuel dump yanajaq anbarı
full dolu
full moon mehtab
full up: I am full up! Mān doymusham.
funeral dāfnetmā mārasimi
funny māzāli
furniture mebel
future gālājāk

G

gallon qalon
game oyun; *match* partiya
gangrene qanqrena
gangster qanqster; quldur
garage qarazh
garden bagh
garbage zibil
garlic sarımsaq
garrison garnizon
gas qaz; *petrol* benzin
gas bottle qaz balonu
gas canister qaz balonu
gas field qaz yataghı
gas production qaz istehsalı
gas well qaz quyusu
gate darvaza
gear ötürüjü, naqil
general *adjective* ümumi
general *noun* general
genitals jinsi orqanlar
genocide soyqırım
geologist geoloq
Georgia Gürjüstan
Georgian Gürjü; *language* Gürjü dilindā
German Alman; *language* Almanja
Germany Almaniya
germs mikrob
get almaq
get up ayagha qalkhmaq; & *see* **wake**
giant div
gift hādiyyā
girl qız
girlfriend qız dostu
give birth doghmaq
give vermāk; **give me ...** mānā .... ver

Gypsy Qarachı
glass *substance* shŭshä; *drinking* stäkan; *small shots* gädäh; **glass of water** bir stäkan su
glasses gözlük
gloves äljäk
go getmäk; **go!**; **let's go!**; **go out** chölä chıkhmaq; **go to bed**
goal *aim* hädäf; *football* qol
goat kechi
God Allah
gold qızıl
golf golf
golf course golf üchün meydancha
good yakhshı
good bye! Sagh ol(un)*!; khudahafiz!
good luck! Ughurlu olsun!
goose qaz
government hökumät
grain tokhum
gram qram
grammar qrammatika
grandchild nävä
grandfather baba
grandmother nänä
grape üzüm
grass ot
grateful: I am grateful. Chokh minnätdaram.
grave *adjective* jiddi
grave *noun* mäzar
gravel jınqıl
great böyük
greatest än böyük
Greek *person* Yunan; *language* Yunanja
green yashil
greengrocer göyärti satan, säbzävatchi
grenade qumbara
grind üyütmäk
ground yer
group qrup
grow boy atmaq
grow crops mähsul yetishtirmäk
grow up böyümäk
guard *noun* mühafizächi; qvardiya; **border guard** särhäddchi; särhädd qoshunları
guard *verb* qorumaq
guerrilla partizan
guest qonaq
guest speaker dä'vät olunmush mä'ruzächi
guesthouse qonaq evi
guide *noun* gid
guide *verb* yol göstärmäk

guidebook turist kitabchası
gum qatran; **chewing gum** saqqız
gun tüfäng
gynecologist ginekolog

H

hair sach
hairbrush daragh
haircut sach käsmäk; **I want a haircut please.** Zähmät olmasa sachımı gödäk edin.
hairdresser bärbär, dälläk
hairdryer fen, sach qurudan
half yarı
hamburger hamburger
hammer chäkij
hand äl
handbag äl chantası
handicraft äl ishi
handle dästäk
hand over tä'fil vermäk
handset dästäy
hang asmaq
hangar anqar
hangover khumarlıq; bashaghrı
happen bash vermäk
happy khoshbäkht
harbour liman
hard *not soft* bärk; *difficult* chätin
hardware store täsärrufat malları dükanı
harmful zärärli
harvest mähsul
hat papagh
hate nifrät etmäk
have malik olmaq
have to -malı/-mäli; **I have to go.** Män getmäliyäm.
hay ot
haystack taya
he o
head bash; *boss* boss
headache bash agrısı
head of state dövlät bashchısı
headquarters mänzilqärargah
heal shäfa vermäk
health saghlamlıq
healthcare sähiyyä
healthy saghlam
hear eshitmäk
heart üräk
heart attack üräk tutması
heart condition üräk khästäliyi
heat *noun* härarät
heating isitmä
heating coil elektrik spiral
heatwave istilik dalghası

heaven sāma
heavy aghır
helicopter helikopter
hell jāhännäm
hello! alo!; salam (āleyküm)! *to which the reply is* (āleyküm) salam!
help *verb* kömäk etmäk; **Can you help me?** Mänä kömäk edä bilärsinizmi?; **Help!** Kömäk edin!
hen toyuq
hepatitis sarılıq khästäliyi
her onun/onu/ona
herb ot bitkisi
herd sürü
here burada
here is ... budur ...
here are ... bunlardır ...
hero qähräman
hers onun
herself onun özü
hide gizlätmäk
high uja; yüksäk; **high blood pressure** yüksäk qan täzyiqi
hill täpä
himself onun özü
Hindu Hindu dindarı
Hinduism Hindu dini
hire kirayä etmäk
his onun/onu/ona
historian tarikhchi
history tarikh
hit vurmaq
hit a mine minaya düshmäk
hold tutmaq
hole deshik
holiday bayram
homeland yurd; vätän
homeless yurdsuz
honey bal
honeymoon bal ayı
hood *of car*
hook qırmaq
horse at
horse racing chıdır
horse-riding at yarışı
hose shlanq
hospital khästäkhana
host sahib
hostage äsir
hostel yataqkhana
hot isti; *spicy* istiotlu
hot water isti su
hotel mehmankhana; otel
hour saat
house ev
housing estate/project kvartal, mähällä

how? nejä?; **how are you?** Nejäsiniz?; **how far?** nä qädär uzagh?; **how many?** nechä dänä?; **how much?** nä qädär?; **how near?** nä qädär yakhın?
however bununla belä
human *adjective* bäshäri
human being insan
human rights insan hüquqlari
humanitarian humanitar
humanitarian aid humanitar yardım
humor yumor
humorous yumoristik
hundred yüz
hungry: I'm hungry. Män ajımısham.
hunt ovlamaq
hurry: I'm in a hurry. Män täläsiräm.
hurt: Where does it hurt? Haranız aghrıyır?; **It hurts here.** Buram aghrıyır.
husband är
hygiene gigiyena; tämizlik

I

I män
ice buz
ice ax buz baltası
ice cream dondurma
I.D. shäkhsiyyät väsiqäsi; **Do you have any I.D.?** Sizdä här hansı bir sänäd varmı?
idea fikir
identification *see* **I.D.**
I.D.P. mäjburi köchkün
if ägär
if possible mümkünsä
ill: I am ill. Män khästäyäm.
illegal qeyri-qanuni
illness khästälik
image shäkil
imam imam
immigrant mühajir
immigration mühajirät
import *verb* idkhal etmäk
importance vajiblik
important mühüm
impossible imkansız
improve täkmilläshdirmäk
in -dä/-da; ichäriyä
in front of qabaghında
included dakhil olmaqla; dakhil edilmish
independence müstäqillik
independent müstäqil
independent state müstäqil dövlät
India Hindistan
Indian Hind

India

indicator light indikator ishıqı
indigestion mә'dә pozqunluqu
industry sәnaye
infant kőrpә
infection infeksiya
influenza qrip
information mәlumat
information office mәlumat bürosu
Ingush Ingush
injure zәdәlәmәk
injured yaralı
injury zәrәr; yara
ink mürәkkәb
inner-tube kamera; shin
innocent günahsız
insane qeyri-normal
inscription yazı
insect hәsharat
insecticide insektisid, qurd dәrmani
instead әvәzinә; yerinә
institute institut
insurance: I have medical insurance.
    Mәnim tibbi sığhortam vardır.
insurance policy sığhorta sәnәdi
**insured: My possessions are
    insured.** Mәnim shәkhsi
    әshyalarım sığhortalanıb.
intend niyyәt etmәk
interest maraq
interesting maraqlı
interior dakhili
internal flight dakhili uchush
Internally Displaced Person mәjburi
    kőchkün
international code beynәlkhalq kod
international flight beynәlkhalq
    uchush
international operator beynәlkhalq
    operator
Internet internet
interpreter tәrjümәchi
interval interval
interview müsahibә
into -ә/-yә
introduce tәqdim etmәk
introduction müqәddimә
invasion ishghal
invention ikhtira
inventor ikhtirachı
investigate arashdırmaq
investigation tәhqiqat
invitation dә'vәtnamә
invite dә'vәt etmәk
Iran Iran
Iranian Iranlı
Ireland Irlandiya
Irish Irlandiyalı

iron polad; *for clothes* ütü
Islam Islam
Israel Israil
it o/onu/ona
Italian *person* Italiyalı; Italiyan
Italian *language* Italyanja
Italy Italiya
itch qashınma
its onunku
itself őzü

J

jack *car* domkrat
jacket penjәk
jade dash
January yanvar
Japan Yaponiya
Japanese *person* Yaponiyalı
Japanese *language* Yaponja
jaw chәnә
jazz jaz
jeans jins
jewelry zәrgәrlik malları
Jew, Jewish Yәhudi
job ish
joke zarafat
journalist zhurnalist
Judaism Yahudi dini
judge hakim
July iyul
jump leads
**jumpstart: Can you jumpstart the
    car?** Itәlәyib mashını ishә sala
    bilәrsәnmi?
June iyun
junior daha gәnj
just as
justice ádalәt

K

Kabardian Kabardin
Kalmuk Kalmık
Karachai Karachay
kebab kәbab
keep sakhlamaq
ketchup kechup
kettle chaynik; qәfәdәn
key achar
kidnap oghurlamaq
kidnapper girov götürәn
kidney bőyrәk
kilim kilim
kill őldürmәk
killer qatil
kilogram kiloqram
kilometer kilometr
kind *adjective* mehriban

kind *noun* növ; **what kind?** hansı növdän?
king kral
kiosk kiosk
kiss öpmäk
kitchen mätbäkh
knee diz
kneel diz chökmäk
knife bıchaq
knock taqqıldatmaq
know bilmäk; **I know.** Män . . . biliräm.; **I don't know.** Män . . . bilmiräm.; **Do you know him/her?** Sän onu tanıyırsanmı?
knowledge bilik
known: tanınan; **well-known** tanınmısh
kolkhoz kolkhoz
Koran Qur'an
Kumyk kumık
Kurd kürd

L

laboratory laboratoriya
lack *verb* chatmamaq
ladder pilläkän
lake göl
lamb quzu
lamp lampa
land yer
landing strip enish
landslide chökmä, torpaq sürüshmäsi
language dil
lap ätäk
laptop computer laptop kompüteri
large böyük
larger daha böyük
last *adjective* akhırınjı; sonunju
last *verb* davam etmäk
late gejikmish; **to be late** gejimäk
laugh *verb* gülmäk
laundry paltaryuyan, paltartämizläyän; yuyulajaq paltar
laundry service paltarın yuyulması khidmäti
law hüquq
law court mähkämä
lawyer hüquqshunas, advokat
lay qoymaq
lay mines mina yatızdırmaq; mina qoymaq
Laz Laz
lazy tänbäl
lead *noun* qurghushun
lead *verb* aparmaq
leader rähbär; lider
leaf yarpaq

leak akhmaq
lean äyilmäk
leap atılmaq
learn öyränmäk
leather däri
leave tärk etmäk
lecture mühazirä
left sol
left-wing solchu; sol-qanadlı
leg bud
legal hüquqi
legend äfsanä
lemon lumu
lend borj vermäk
lengthen uzunluq
lens linza; **contact lenses** linzalar
less daha az
lesson därs
letter mäktub
lettuce kahı
level *adjective* üfqi
level *noun* säviyyä
lever qol
Lezgian läzgi
liberation azadetmä
library kitabkhana
lie *noun* uydurma; yalan
lie down uzanmaq
life häyat
lift *elevator* lift
lift *verb* qaldırmaq
light *adjective: not dark* ıshıqlı; *not heavy* yüngül
light *noun* ishıq; **Do you have a light?** Alıshqan varmı?
light *verb* yandırmaq; **May we light a fire?** Biz od qalaya bilärikmi?
lightbulb lampa
light meter ishıq güjünü ölchän jihaz
lighter alıshqan
lighter fluid alıshqan yanajaqı
lighting ishıq jihazi
lightning shimshäk
like . . . kimi; **like that** o kimi; **like this** bu kimi
like *verb* sevmäk; **I like . . . . . .** mänim khoshuma gälir; **I don't like . . . . . .** mänim khoshuma gälmir
likely deyäsän
limbs äl-ayaq
lime ähäng
limit hädd
line khätt
linguist dilchi
linguistics dilchilik
lip dodaq
lipstick dodaq pomadası

list siyahı
listen qulaq asmaq
liter litr
literature ädäbiyyat
little balaja; kichik; **a little bit** bir az
live yashamaq
liver qarajiyär
lizard kärtänkälä
loaf bulka
local yerli
location yer
lock kılıd
locomotive lokomotiv; aparıjı qatar
long uzun
look bakhmaq; görünmäk
look for akhtarmaq
loose change khırda pul
lose: I have lost ... Män ...
    itirmishäm.; **I have lost my key.**
    Män otaghımın acharını
    itirmishäm.; **I am lost.** Män
    yolumu itirmishäm.
lost see **lose**
lot, a lot bir chokh
loud bärk
loudly ujadan
louse bit
love noun mähäbbät; sevgi
love verb sevmäk
low ashaghı
low blood pressure ashaqı qan täzyiqi
LP val
luck: good luck! ughur olsun!
lunch noun nahar
lunch verb nahar etmäk
lung agh jiyär

M

machine mashın
machine gun güllä sachan; pulemyot
madrasa mädräsä
mafia mafiya
magazine därgi, zhurnal
magnetic maqnitli
mail pocht
mailbox pocht qutusu
main äsas
main square bash meydan
maintain müdafiä etmäk
maize qarghıdalı
majority chokhluq
make etmäk
make-up kosmetika
male noun kishi
male adjective kishi
mammal mämäli
man kishi

manager müdir
manual book soraq kitabchası
manual worker fählä
many bir chokh; **too many**
    häddindän artigh chokh; **how
    many?** nä qädär?; nechä?
map khäritä; **map of Baku** Bakının
    khäritäsi
March mart
mare madyan
marital status ailä väziyyäti
mark nishan; currency marka
market bazar
marriage evlänmä
married: I am married. female Män
    ärdäyäm./male Män evliyam.
marsh qamıshlıq
martyr shähid
mascara sürmä
massacre qırghın; soyqırım
match football partiya
matches kibrit
material material
mathematics riyazıyyat
matter: It doesn't matter. Bu vajib
    deyil./Bir shey deyil.
mattress döshäk (pronounced
    döshäy)
mausoleum mavsoley
May may
may I? olarmı?
maybe bälkä
me mänä/mäni
meal yemäk
meals yemäklär
mean verb mä'nası olmaq
meaning mä'na
measure verb ölchmäk
meat ät
mechanic mekhanik
media mätbuat
medical tibbi
medical insurance tibbi sığorta
medication därman
medicine täbabät
meet görüshmäk
meeting görüsh
melon yemish
member üzv
memory yaddash
menthol mentollu
menu menyu
mercenary muzdur
message khäbär
metal metal
meter metr
metro metro

microscope mikroskop
middle orta
middle name atanızın adı
midnight gecä yarısı
midsummer yayın ortası
midwife mama häkimi
midwinter qıshın ortası
mild winter yumshaq qısh
mile mil
military härbi
milk süd
mill däyirman
millet darı
million milyon
minaret minarä
mine *adjective* mänimki
mine detector mina tapan
mine disposal mina tämizläyiji
mine *mineral* shakhta; mädän;
    explosive mina
minefield minalanmısh sahä
miner shakhtachı
mineral mineral
mineral water mineral su
Mingrelian Mınqrel
minister nazir
ministry nazirlik
Ministry of Agriculture Känd
    Täsärrufatı Nazirliyi
Ministry of Defense Müdafiä
    Nazirliyi
Ministry of Education Tähsil
    Nazirliyi
Ministry of Foreign Affairs Khariji
    İshlär Nazirliyi
Ministry of Health Sähiyyä Nazirliyi
Ministry of Home Affairs Dakhili
    İshlär Nazirliyi
Ministry of Justice Ädliyyä Nazirliyi
Ministry of Transport Näqliyyat
    Nazirliyi
minority azlıq
minute *noun* däqiqä
miracle möjüzä
mirror güzgü
Miss Khanım
missile raket
mist duman
mistake sähv; **to make a mistake**
    sähv etmäk
misty dumanlı
misunderstand düz basha
    düshmämäk
mobile phone jib telefonu; mobil telefon
model *fashion* model; maneken
modem modem
modern müasir

moment an; moment
monarch kral
monastery monastır
Monday bazar ertäsi
money pul
monk rahib
month ay
monument mä'bäd
moon ay; **full moon** mehtab; **new
    moon** täzä ay
more daha chokh
more or less az-chokh
morning sähär; **good morning!**
    Sabahın(ız)* kheyir!; **this morning**
    bu sähär
mosque mäsjid
mosquito aghjaqanad
most än chokh
mother ana
motorbike motosiklet
mountain dagh
Mountain Jew Tat
mountain pass dagh yolu; ashırım
mouse sichan
mouth aghız
mouthwash aghız üchün qar-qara
    därmanı
move köchmäk
movie film; **the movies** kino
Mr. Jänäb
Mrs. Khanım
Ms. Khanım
much chokh; **not much** chokh deyil;
    az; **too much** häddindän artıgh
    chokh; **how much?** Nä qädär?;
    how much is it? Bu nechäyädir?
mud palchıq
mule qatır
mullah molla
murder *noun* qätl
murder *verb* öldürmäk; qätlä
    yetirmäk
murderer qatil
museum muzey
music musiqi
Muslim müsälman
must *see* have to
mustache bığh
mustard khardal
my mänim
myself özüm

N

Nagorno-Karabakh Daghlıq Qarabagh
nail qadagh; **finger nail** dırnaq
nail-clippers dırnaq qaychisi
Nakhichevan Nakhchıvan

name ad; **surname** soyad; familiya;
  What is your name? Adınız nädir?
  — **My name is Fred.** Adım Freddir.
napkin älsilän; khoräk däsmalı
narrow dar
nation *state* dövlät; *people* khalq
nationality millät; *& see* citizenship
natural täbii
natural disaster täbii fälakät
natural resources täbii ehtiyatlar
nature täbiät
navy däniz donanması
near yakhın
nearby yakhında yerläshän
nearly demäk olar ki; azqala
necessary: it's necessary lazımdır; bu
  lazımdır
neck boyun
necklace boyunbaghı; hämail
necktie qalstuk
need ehtiyajı olmaq; **I need...**
  Mänim...-ä/a ehtiyajim var.;
  Mänä... lazımdır
needle iynä
negotiator danıshıqları aparan shäkhs
neighbor qonshu
neither...nor nä...nä
nerve äsäb
net tor
neutral drive neytral
never hech vakht
new täzä; yeni
new moon täzä ay
news khäbärlär
New Year *March 21* Novruz; *January 1*
  Yeni İl Bayramı
New Zealand Yeni Zelandiya
news agency khäbärlär agentliyi
newspaper qäzet; **newspaper in
  English** ingilisjä qäzet
newsstand qäzet dükanı
next növbäti
next week gälän häftä
nice yakhshı
night gejä; **good night!** Gejän(iz)*
  kheyrä qalsın!
nightclub gejä klubu; diskoteka
nine doqquz
nineteen on doqquz
ninety dokhsan
no kheyr; yokh; **no entry** girish
  gadaghandır; **no smoking** siqaret
  chäkmäk qodaghandır; **no sugar,
  please** shäkärsiz, zähmät olmasa
nobody hech käs
Nogai Noqay
noise säs-küy

noisy säs-küylü
noon günorta
no one hech käs
nor: neither...nor nä...nä
normal normal
north *noun* shimal
Northern Ireland Shimali İrlandiya
northern *adjective* shimali
nose burun
not yokh; deyil; **do not...!** ...etmä!
not enough kifayät deyil; qeyri-kafi
note: bank note kaghız pulu
notebook kitabcha
nothing hech nä
nought sıfır
noun isim
novel roman; **novels in English**
  ingilisjä romanlar
November noyabr
now indi
nowhere hech yerä
nuclear power nüvä qüvväsi;
  political nüvä dövlät
nuclear power station nuvä elektrik
  stansiyası
number miqdar; nömrä
nun rahibä
nurse tibb bajısı
nut qoz

O

oak palıd
obligation öhdälik
observer müshahidächi
occasion münasibät
occupation *job* ish; *of a country*
  ishghal
occupying forces ishghalchı qüvvälär
occur bash vermäk
o'clock: It is...o'clock. Saat... dir.
October oktyabr
of course älbättä
off-shore dänizdä
office ofis
officer *military* zabit
office worker ofis ishchisi
often tez-tez
oil neft; *cooking* yagh
oilcan yagh bankası
oilfield neft yataghı; neft mä'däni
oil pipeline neft kämäri
oil production neft istehsalı
oil refinery neft ayırma müässisäsi
oil slick neft läkäsi
oil spill neft akhını
oil tanker neft tankeri
oil well neft quyusu

oil worker neftchi
old goja; köhnä; **How old are you?**
　Nechä yashın(ız*) var?; **I am . . .**
　years old. Mänim . . . yashım var.
Old City köhnä shähär; *(in Baku)*
　İchäri Shähär
on -da/-dä; **on time** vakhtında
once bir däfä
one bir
one-way street birtäräfli häräkät
　küchäsi
one-way ticket bir basha bilet
only *adjective* yeganä; *adverb* täkjä
onto üstünä
open *adjective* achıq
open *verb* achmaq
opera opera
opera house opera teatrı
operating theater järrahiyyä
　ämäliyyatı otaghı
operation *surgical* järrahiyyä
　ämäliyyatı
operator operator; **telephone**
　operator telefonchu
opposite üzbäüz; äksına
opposition mükhalifät
or vä ya; yakhud
orange *fruit* portaghal; *colour* narınjı
orchard bagh
order *noun* ämr
order *someone* ämr etmäk; *a meal*
　sifarish etmäk
ordinary adi
origin mänbä
original orizhinal
orphan yetim
Orthodox pravoslav khristian
Ossete Osetiyalı
Ossetia Osetiya
other digär; o biri
ounce untsiya
our; ours bizim
ourselves özümüz
out kharijä
outside *adjective* bayır
overcoat palto; kürk
overtake
owl bayqush
own *adjective* öz(ünün)
own *verb* malik olmaq; sahib olmaq
oxygen oksigen

P

package baghlama; paket
padlock anbar kiliti, qıfıl
pain aghrı
painkiller aghrıkäsän därman

painkillers aghrıkäsän därmanlar
paint *noun* boya
paint *verb* boyamaq
painter rässam
painting shäkil
Pakistan Pakistan
Pakistani pakistanlı
palace saray
pale sönük
paper *substance* kaghız; *newspaper*
　qäzet; *article* mäqalä; **a piece of**
　paper (bir parcha) kaghız
parachute parashut
paradise jännät
paralyze paralich olmaq
parcel baghlama
parents valideynlär
park *noun* park
park *verb* sakhlamaq
parliament parlament; *Azerbaijani*
　Milli Mäjlis
part hissä
participate ishtirak etmäk
partridge käklik
party shänlik; qonaghlıq; *political*
　siyasi partiya
pass *verb* kechmäk; *and see*
　mountain pass
passable: **Is the road passable?** Bu
　yolnan kechmäk mümkündürmü?
passenger särnishin
passport pasport
passport number pasportun nömräsi
past *adjective* kechmish
past *noun* kechmish
pasta khämir yemäyi (garnir)
path jıghır
patient *medical* pasient; khästä
pay *noun* muzd
pay *verb* ödämäk
payment ödämä
peace sülh
peace talks sülh danıshıqları
peace-keeping troops sülhü-
　qoruyuju qüvvälär
peach shaftalı
peak zirvä; pik
pear armud
pearl mirvari
peasant kändli
pediatrician pediatr; ushaq häkimi
pediatrics pediatriya
pelvis chanaq sümüyü
pen qäläm
pencil karandash
penicillin penisilin
penknife jib bıjaqı

people insanlar; adamlar; khalq; ähali;
    familiar jamaat
pepper istiot
perfect tam
perform oynamaq; ifa etmäk
performance tamasha
perfume ätir
perhaps bälkä
period period; müddät
Persian *person* fars; iranlı
Persian *thing* fars
person shäkhs
petrol benzin
petroleum neft
pharmacy äjzachıkhana; aptek
phone *noun* telefon
phone *verb* zäng etmäk
phonetics fonetika
photo foto shäkil
photocopier kopiya mashını; sürät
    chıkharma mashını; kseroks
photocopy fotosürät
photographer fotoqrafchı
photography fotoqrafiya; fotosänät
physics fizika
physiotherapy fizioterapiya
piano piano
pickax külüng
picture shäkil; räsm
pig donuz
pilgrim ziyarätchı; zävvar; *to Mecca*
    hajjı
pill häb
pillow bashaltı
pilot pilot
pin sanjaq
pine sham aghajı
pink chährayı
pins and needles *medical* ayaghım
    yatmıshdır
pipe *tube* boru; *smoking* qälyan
pistachio pestä
pistol tapanja
pitch meydan
pizza pitsa
place yer
place of birth anadan olan yer;
    doghum yeri
plain *noun* düzänlik
plane täyyarä
plank shalban
plant bitki
planting äkin; säpin
plastic plastmas
plate boshqab
platform platforma
platform number platforma nömräsi

play *theater* pyes
play *verb* oynamaq; *musical
    instrument* chalmaq
please! *asking* khahish ediräm!;
    lütfän!; *inviting* buyurunuz!
pleasure häzz
plow *noun* kotan
plow *verb* shumlamaq
plug *bath* tıkhaj; *electric* razetka
plum gavali; sour plum alcha
p.m. akhsham vakhtı
pocket jib
podium podium
poem poema
poet shair
poison zähär
police polis
police station polis shö'bäsi
policeman polis näfäri (ishchisi)
polite näzakätli
political siyasi
political scientist politolog
politician siyasätchi
politics siyasät
pollution ätraf mühitin chirklänmäsi
pomegranate nar
pony poni
pool hovuz
poor yokhsul
population ähali
pork donuz
port liman
portable TV balaja televizor; äl
    televizoru
portion pay
portrait portret
possible ehtimal ki; ola bilär; if
    possible mümkündürsä
position väziyyät
post office pocht
postcard pocht kartı
potato kartof
pottery duluschu äshyaları
pound funt
pour tökmäk
pour out sızmaq
P.O.W. härbi äsir
P.O.W. camp härbi äsirlär düshärgäsi
powder toz
power qüvvä
praise tä'rif
pray dua etmäk
prefer üstün tutmaq
pregnant: hamilä; boylu; I'm
    pregnant. Män hamiläyäm.
premier bash nazir
prepare hazırlamaq

present *adjective* indiki
present *time* mövjud; *gift* hädiyyä
president prezident
presidential guard prezident qvardiyası
pressure tazyiq; **high blood pressure** hipertoniya; **low blood pressure** hipotoniya
previously ävvälär
price qiymät
pride iftikhar
priest keshish
prime minister bash nazir
principle prinsip
print chap etmäk
printer *computer* printer; kompyuter chap mashını
prison häbskhana
prisoner äsir
prize priz; mükafat
probable mümkündür; **it is probable** bu mümkündür
probably mümkündür
problem problem; **no problem!** problem deyil!
product mähsul
profession peshä
professional mütäkhässis
professor professor
program proqram; **radio program** radio verilishi
projector proyektor
pronounce täläffüz etmäk
pronounciation täläffüz
proof sübut
prosthesis protez
protect qorumaq
protection qorunma
protest *noun* e'tiraz
protest *verb* e'tiraz etmäk
proud mäghrur
prove sübut etmäk
proverb zärb-mäsäl
pub piväkhana, pab
public phone telefon-avtomat
publish näshr etmäk
publisher nashir
pull dartmaq
pump *noun* nasos; soruyuju
pump *verb* chäkmäk
pumping station nasos mäntäqäsi
pumpkin balqabaq
puncture deshik; **I have a puncture.** Täkär deshilib.
punish jäzalandırmaq
pupil shagird
purple bänövshäyi
push itälämäk

put qoymaq
put on clothes paltar geymäk
put through on the phone jalashdırmaq

Q

quarter rüb; *area* kvartal; **one-quarter** dörddäbir; **three-quarters** dördäüch
queen kralichä
question sual
quick tez
quickly tezliklä
quiet *adjective* sakit
quietly sakitjä
quilt yorghan
quit tärk etmäk
Qur'an Qur'an

R

rabbit dovshan
rabies quduzluq
radar radar
radiator radiator
radio radio
radio broadcast radioyayımı
radio program radio verilish
radio station radio stansiyası
radio taxi radiolu taksi
raid hüjum; reyd
railway dämir yolu
railway station dämir yolu stansiyası
rain yaghısh
rainbow qöy qurshaghı
rain: it is raining yaghısh yaghır
rainy weather yaghmurlu hava
raise qaldırmaq
ram qoch
Ramadan Ramazan Bayramı
range mäsafä
rape zorlama; **I've been raped.** Mäni zorlayıblar.
rapid chevik
rapidly chevik
rat sichovul
rate: What is the exchange rate? Däyishmä mäzännäsi nädir?
ravage *verb* daghıtmaq
ravine yarghan
raw chiy
razor üzqırkhma jihazı
razorblade üzqırkhma ülgüjü
reactionary irtijachı
read okhumaq
ready hazır; **I am ready.** Män haziram.
real äsl

ready

realize: anlamaq; **I didn't realize anything was wrong.** Män näyinsä düz olmadığhını anlamadım.
reality reallıq
reaping bichin
reason äsas; säbäb; **for that reason** bu säbäbdän
reason for travel säfärin mäqsädi
rebel noun üsyanchı
receipt qäbz
receive almaq
recently son zamanlar
reception desk qavrama
recognize tanımaq
record noun yazı; musiqi yazısı; sports rekord; document qeyd
record verb lentä yazmaq
Red Cross Qırmızı Khach
red qırmızı
referee hakim
refine e'mal etmäk
refinery e'malatkhana; **oil refinery** neftayırma muässisäsi
refrigerator soyuduju
refugee qachqın
refugee camp qachqın düshärgäsi
refugees qachqınlar
regime rezhim
region rayon; ärazi; bölgä
registered mail sifarishli mäktub
reign noun hökmranlıq
relationship qohumluq
relative qohum
relatives qohum-äqräbä
relax dinjälmäk
release azad etmäk; burakhmaq
relief aid yardım
religion din
remain qalmaq
remember yadda sakhlamaq
repair noun tä'mir
repair verb tä'mir etmäk
reparation reparasiya
repeat täkrar etmäk
replace yerinä qoymaq; däyishmäk
reply javab vermäk
report hesabat; khäbär
represent tämsil etmäk
representation nümayändälik; tämsilchilik
representative nümayändä; tämsilchi
republic respublika
research tädqiqat
reservation: I have a reservation. Mänim otaghım sifarish olunub.
reserve sifarish etmäk; **Can I reserve**
a place? Män yer sifarish edä bilärämmı?
reserved sifarish edilib
reserves ehtiyatlar
rest noun istirahät; others yerdä qalanlar
rest verb istirahät etmäk
restaurant restoran
return qayıtmaq
return ticket iki basha bilet
reverse adjective dal ötürüjüsü
reverse verb dala vermäk
review newspaper ijmal; mäjmüä
revolution inqilab
rice düyü
rich zängin
ride a horse at sürmäk
rifle tüfäng
right side sagh; correct; **You are right.** Siz haqlısınız!; **the right amount** lazımı qädär
right-wing saghchır; sagh-qanadlı
rights haqqlar; **civil rights** vätändash haqqları; **human rights** insan haqqları
ring noun üzük
ring verb zäng etmäk; **I want to ring . . .** Män . . . zäng etmäk istäyiräm.
riot qalmaqal; dara
ripe yetishmish
rise durmaq
risk risq
river chay
riverbank chay sahili
road yol
road map yol khäritäsi; yol atlası
roadblock yol postu
rob soymaq; **I've been robbed.** Mäni soyublar.
robbery qarätchilik
rock dash; qaya
rock 'n' roll rok-end-rol
rock concert rok konserti
roof dam
room otaq; **single room** bir näfärlik otaq; **double room** iki näfärlik otaq
room number otaghın nömräsi
room service otaghı tämizlämä khidmäti
rooster khoruz
rope kämär
rosary täsbeh
rose qızıl gül
route yol
row line khätt
royal kral
rubber rezin

rubbish zibil
ruble rubl
rude kobud
rug khalcha
rugby reqbi
ruins daghıntılar
ruler *person* hökmdar; *measure* khätkesh
run qachmaq
run out qurtarmaq; **I have run out of gas.** Yanajaghım qurtarib.
Russia Rusiya
Russian *person* rus
Russian *language* ruscha
rust pas

S

sack kisä
sad qämli
safe *adjective* sagh-salamat
safe box seyf
safety tählükäsizlik
safety pin sanjaq
saffron
saint müqäddäs
saint's tomb seyyidin mäzarı
salad salat
salesperson satıjı
salon *shop* salon
salt duz
salty duzlu
samovar samavar
sand qum
sandwich buterbrod
satellite peyk
satellite phone peyk telefonu
satisfactory kafi; qane ediji
satisfied razı
Saturday shänbä
sausage kalbasa
save *rescue* khilas etmäk; *money* pul yıghmaq
saw *noun* mishar
saw *verb* misharlamaq
say demäk
scarf shärf
scatter daghıtmaq
school mäktäb
science elm
scientific elmi
scientist elmi ishchi; tädqiqatchı
scissors qaychı
score: **What's the score?** Hesab nechä oldu?; **Who scored?** Kim qol vurdu?
Scotland Shotlandiya
Scottish *person* shotland
screw vint

screwdriver vintburan
scythe düriz
sea däniz
search akhtarmaq
season mövsum, fäsil
seat oturajaq
seat *political* yer
second *adjective* ikinji
second *noun* saniyä
second class ikinji klas; ikinji däräjä
second-hand ishlänmish
secret *adjective* gizli
secret *noun* sirr
secret police mäkhfi polis
secretary *male* katib; *female* katibä
section seksiya; bölmä
security tählükäsizlik
see görmäk
seed tokhum; takhıl
seek akhtarmaq
seismic survey seysmolozhi tädqiqat
seize zäbt etmäk
self özü
sell satmaq
send göndärmäk
senior daha yashlı
sense hiss
September sentyabr
septic septik; irinli
series silsilä
serious jiddi
service khidmät
session sessiya; ijlas
seven yeddi
seventeen on yeddi
seventy yetmish
several bir nechä
severe winter aghır qısh
sew tikmäk
sex jinsiyyät; seks
shade kölgä
shah shah; padshah
shake titrätmäk; titrämäk
shampoo shampun
shape shekil; chevrä
share *verb* bölüshmäk
sharp iti
shaving cream üzqırkhma kremi
she o
sheep qoyun
sheepdog chobaniti, alabash
sheet mäläfä
shell *of nut* qabıgh; *military* märmi; *sea* qın
shelter sığınajaq
shepherd choban
shine parlamaq

ship gämi
shirt köynäk
shock *medical* shok
shoes tufli; ayaqqabı
shoeshop ayaqqabı dükanı
shoot atäsh achmaq; **don't shoot!** atäsh achmayın!
shop maghaza; dükan
shopkeeper dükanchı
shopping maghazaları gäzmäk
shore sahil
short alchaq
shortage qıtlıq
shoulder chiyin
shout chıghırrnaq
shovel küräk
show *noun* tamasha
show *verb* göstärmäk
shower dush
shrapnel qälpä
shrine ibadätgah, müqäddäs yer
shut *adjective* baghlı
shut *verb* baghlamaq
sick khästä; **I am sick.** Män khästälänmishäm.
sidestreet yan küchä
sight mänzärä
sign *noun* isharä
signature imza
sign an agreement imzalamaq
significance ähämiyyät
significant vajib
silence sükut
silent sässiz
silk ipäk
silly akhmaq
silver gümüsh
similar okhshar
since . . .-dän bäri
sing mahnı okhumaq
single täk; **single room** täk otaq; bir näfärlik otaq; **I am single.** Män subayam.
sink *noun* tas
sink *verb* batmaq
sister bajı
sit oturmaq
situation väziyyät
six altı
sixteen on altı
sixth altınjı
sixty altmış
size ölchü; *quantity* häjm
skating konki sürmäk
ski slope khizäk enishi
skiing ayaq khizäyi idmanı
skilift qaldırıjı kran

skill qabiliyyät
skilled qabiliyyätli
skin däri
sky säma; göy
sleep *noun* yukhu
sleep *verb* yatmaq
sleeping bag yataqlı torba
sleeping car yataq vaqonu
sleeping pill(s) yukhu därmanı
sleepy: I am sleepy. Män yukhuluyam.
sleet boran
sling *medical* sarıma
slip sürüshmäk
slope daghın döshü; yamaj
slow yavash
slowly yavashja
small balaja; kichik
smaller daha balaja/kichik
smell *noun* qokhu
smoke *noun* duman; tüstü
smoke *verb* tüstülämäk
smoking siqaret chäkmäk
smuggler qachaqmalchı
snack qalyanaltı
snail ilbiz
snake ilan
snakebite ilan dishlämäsi
snow qar
snow: It is snowing. Qar yaghır.
snowdrift qar yaghını; qar täpäsi
so belä
so much/many qädär
soap sabun
soccer futbol
soccer match futbol matchı
social sosial
socialism sosializm
socialist *adjective* sosialist
socialist *noun* sosialist
society jämiyyät
sock jorab
socks jorablar
soft yumshaq
soldier äskär
solstice sırsıra; buz baghlama
solve häll etmäk
some bä'zi
somehow nejäsä
someone/somebody birisi; kimsä
something bir shey
sometimes bä'zän
somewhere harasa
son oghul
song mahnı; näghmä
soon bu yakhında; tezliklä
sore throat boghaz agrısı

sorry! *familiar* baghıshla!; *formal* üzr istäyiräm; **I'm sorry.** Män täässüf ediräm.
soul ruh
sound säs
sound equipment säs yazma avadanlığı
soup shorba; sup
sour tursh
sour plum alcha
source mänbä
south *noun* jänub
southern jänubi
souvenir *shop* suvenir dükanı; hädiyyälär maghazası
Soviet Union Sovet İttifaqı
soviet sovet
sow tokhum etmäk
spa kurort
space yer
spade yaba
Spanish *person* ispaniyalı; *language* ispanja
spanner achar
spare tire ehtiyaj täkäri
sparkling qazlı
speak: Do you speak English? Siz İngilisjä danışırsınızmı?
speak: I speak . . . Män . . . danışıram.
speaker sädr; *parliament* spiker
specialist mütäkhässis
speed sürät
spell: How do you spell that? Bu söz nejä säslänir?
spend khärjlämäk
spicy *hot* istiotlu
spider hörümchäk
spill tökmäk
spin härlätmäk
spine *back* onurgha
spit tüpürmäk
splint *medical* shin
split yarmaq
spoil korlamaq
sponge sunkär
spoon qashiq
sports idman
sportsman sportsmen; idmanchı
spread yaymaq
spring *season* yaz; *water* bulaq suyu; *metal* yay
spy jasus
square: town square meydan
stadium stadion
staff ishchi heyyäti; **General Staff** Bash Qärargah

stage sähnä
stale köhnä; bayat
stallion ayghır
stamp *postal* marka; *official* möhür
stand dözmäk
star ulduz
state *nation* dövlät; *in federation* shtat; *condition* hal
station stansiya
stationer's däftärkhana malları maghazası
stationery däftärkhana lävazimatı
statue heykäl
stay dayanmaq
steak bifshteks
steal oghurlamaq
steal: My . . . has been stolen. Mänim ... oghurlanıb.
steel polad
steering wheel sükan
sterling funt sterlinq
stethoscope stetoskop
stick *noun* däyänäk
stick *verb* yapıshdırmaq
still *adverb* hälä
sting *verb* sanjmaq
stink *verb* iy vermäk
stitches *surgical* tikishlär
stolen: My car has been stolen. Mänim mashınımı qachırdıblar.
stomach qarın; gödän
stomachache qarın aghrısı
stone dash
stop sakhlamaq; sakhla!; **don't stop!** sakhlama!
store anbar; *shop* maghaza
storm fırtına
story hekäyä
stove ojaq
straight: straight: düz; **straight on** düz; **Go straight ahead.** Düz sür.
strange äjaib
stranger gälmä
strawberry chiyäläk; **wild strawberry** böyürtkän
stream akhın
street küchä
strength qüvvät
stretcher khäräk
strike *from work* tä'til
strike *verb* tä'til etmäk
string tilov ipi; tel
strong güjlü
structure struktur
struggle mübarizä
stuck: Our car is stuck. Mashınımız ilishib qalıb.

student täläbä
study *noun* tähsil
study *verb* okhumaq; öyränmäk
subject mövzu
submachine gun avtomat
suburb shähärätrafı qäsäbä
subway *metro* yeraltı kechid
success ughur
such bu kimi
suddenly birdän-birä
sufficient kafi; yararlı
sugar qänd
suit kostyum
suitable uyghun
suitcase chamadan
sultan sultan
summer yay
summit zirvä
summit conference zirvä görüshü
sun günäsh
sunblock cream günäsh shualarına
   qarshı krem
Sunday bazar
sunglasses qunä qarshı eynäk
sunny günäshli
sunny: It is sunny. Günäshlidir.
sunrise gündoghan
sunscreen *see* **sunblock**
sunset qurub; günbatan
supermarket univermaq;
   supermarket
supper sham yemäyi
supply *noun* täjhizat
sure *adjective* ämin; *adverb* shübhäsiz
surgeon järrah
surgery *operation* järrahiyyä
   ämäliyyatı
surname familiya
surprising tääjjüb ediji
swallow *verb* udmaq
Svan Svan
swamp bataghlıq
swear *oath* and ichmäk; *curse* söyüsh
   söymäk
sweat tärlämäk
sweater sviter; yun köynäk
sweep süpürmäk
sweet shirin
sweet pepper bibär
swell shishmäk
swim üzmäk
swimming üzmä
swimming pool hovuz
swing sallanmaq
switch *electric* elektrik düymäsi
switch off söndürmäk
switch on yandırmaq

symbol rämz; simvol
symphony simfoniya
symptom simptom
synagogue sinaqoq
syntax sintaksis
syringe iynä
system sistem

T

table masa; stol
tablecloth süfrä
tablet häb
take götürmäk
**take off: What time does the plane
   take off?** Täyyarä nä zaman qalkhır?
take-out chıkhartmaq
talk danıshmaq
tall uja
Talysh Talısh
tampon tıkhaj; piltä; tampon
tank bak; *military* tank
tap *faucet* kran
tape cassette kaset
tape-recorder maqnitofon
taste *noun* lazzät; dad
taste *verb* dadmaq
tasteless dadsız
tasty dadlı
Tat tat
tax *noun* vergi
tax *verb* vergi qoymaq
tax-free rüsümsüz
tax-free zone vergidän azad ärazi
taxi taksi; **radio taxi** radiolu taksi
tea chay; **tea with lemon** lumulu
   chay; **tea with milk** südlü chay
teach öyrätmäk
teacher *male* müällim; *female*
   müällimä
team komanda
tear *noun* göz yashı
tear *verb* yırtmaq
tear gas gözyashardıjı
teaspoon chay qashığı
technique tekhnika
teeth dishlär
telecommunications televiziya
   ishchisi
telegram teleqram
telephone *noun* telefon; **satellite
   phone** peyk telefonu
telephone *verb* zäng etmäk
telephone center telefon
   danıshıqları märkäzi
telephone operator telefonchu
telephone station telefon stansiyası
telescope teleskop

television televizor
television station televiziya
stansiyası
telex teleks
tell demäk; **tell him/her** ona de; **tell
me** mänä de
temperature qızdırma; **I have a temperature.** Mänim qızdırmam var.
temple mä'bäd
ten on
tennis tenis
tent chadır
tent pegs payachıq
tenth onunju
termite qarışka
terrible qorkhunj; dähshätli
territory ärazi
test *noun* test; yokhlama; sınaq
text mätn
than -dan/-dän
thank täshäkkür etmäk
thank you! Sag ol(un);* täshäkkür
ediräm!
that *preposition* o; *conjunction* ki
that's enough! bu käfayätdir!; bäsdir!
thaw *noun* yumshaq hava
thaw *verb* ärimäk
theater teatr
theft oghurluq
their; theirs onların
themselves özläri
then onda
theory teoriya
there orada
there is/are orada var
therefore onun üchün
thermometer termometr;
istilikölchän
these bunlar
they onlar
thick *wide* enli; *dense* sarsagh;
aghılsız
thief oghru
thin nazik
thing shey
think düshünmäk; zännn etmäk; **I
think . . .** Zännimjä . . .; Fikrimjä . . .
third *adjective* üchünjü; **one-third**
üchdäbir
thirsty: I'm thirsty. Män
sustamısham.
thirteen on üch
thirty otuz
this bu
those onlar
thought fikir
thousand min

thread sap
three üch
three times üch däfä
throat boghaz
thrombosis tromboz
throne takht
through arasından
throw tullamaq
thumb böyük barmaq
thunder göy gurultusu
thunderstorm tufan
Thursday jümä akhshamı
tick *insect* känä
ticket bilet; **one-way ticket** birtäräfli
bilet; **return ticket** ikitäräfli bilet
ticket office bilet kassası
tie *necktie* qalstuk
tie *verb* baghlamaq
ties: diplomatic ties diplomatik
älaqälär
tights qadın jorabları
time vakht; **two times** iki däfä; **for a
long time** chokhdan; **free time**
bosh vakht; **What time is it?** Saat
nechädir?
timetable jädväl
tire *noun* täkär; shin
tire *verb* yorulmaq
tired yorghun
tissues däsmallar
transfer on the phone jalashdırmaq
toast *bread* tost; *drink* saghlıq
tobacco tütün
today bugün
toe daban
together birlikdä; bärabär
toilet ayaghyolu
toilet paper tualet kaghızı
toilet(s) tualet; ayaghyolu
toiletries qiqiyena lävazimatı
token *coin* zheton
tomato pamidor
tomb mäzar
tomorrow sabah; **the day after
tomorrow** birisi gün
tongue dil
tonight bu akhsham
too . . . chokh; *& see also*
too little häddindän artıgh az
too many/much häddindän artıgh
chokh
tools alätlär
tooth dish
toothache dish agrısı
toothbrush dish shötkası
toothpaste dish pastası
toothpick dish üchün chöp
top zirvä

torture *noun* ishgänjä
torture *verb* ishgänjä vermäk
tourism turizm
tourist office turist idaräsi
tourist turist
tourniquet turniket
tow rope baghlama
tow: Can you tow us? Bizi yedäyä ala bilärsinizmi?
towel däsmal
tower bürj; güllä
town shähär
town center shähär märkäzi
town hall ratusha
track yol
tractor traktor
trade union hämkarlar ittifaqı
tradition än'änä
traditional än'änävi
traffic lights svetofor
traffic police yol polisi
train qatar
train station dämir yolu stansiyası
tranquilizer sakitläshdiriji; aghrıkäsän
transformer transformator; kechiriji
transfusion: blood transfusion qanköchürmä
translate tärjümä etmäk
translation tärjümä
translator tärjümächi
transmit verilmäk
transmitter radioveriji aparat
transport näqliyyat
trap tälä
trash zibil
trauma khäsarät; travma
travel agent turist agentiyi
travel *noun* säyahät
travel *verb* säyahät etmäk
traveler säyahätchi
travelers' checks bank chekläri
treacherous khain
treasury khäzinä
tree aghaj
trial *legal* mähkämä
trolley bus troleybus
troops qoshunlar
trouble: What's the trouble? Nä bash verib?
trousers shalvar
truce barıshıq
truck äl arabası
true häqiqi
trunk *of car*
truth häqiqät
try jähd etmäk
tsar char
tube tübik

Tuesday chärshänbä akhshamı
tunnel tünel
Turk Türk
Turkey Türkiyä
turkey hindushka; hind toyughu
Turkish Türk
Turkish baths hamam
Turkish türkjä
turn dönmäk; **turn left!** sola dön!; **turn right!** sagha dön!
twelve on iki
twenty iyirmi
twice iki däfä
twins äkizlär
two iki
two-thirds üchdäiki
type *noun* tip
typewriter chap mashını

U

Ukraine Ukrayna
Ukrainian *language* Ukrayna dilindä
ulcer yara; *stomach ulcer* mä'dä yarası
umbrella chätir
uncle ämi; dayı
uncomfortable narahat
under *prep* altında; *adverb* az
underground yeraltı; *metro* metro
understand bash düshmäk; **I understand** Män anlayıram./Män basha düshüräm; **I don't understand.** Män basha düshmüräm./Män anlamıram.
undertake täshäbbüs etmäk
underwear alt paltar
undo achmaq; pozmaq
UNDP B.M.T.-nin İkishaf Proqramı
unemployed avara; ishsiz
unemployment ishsizlik
UNESCO Yunesko; BMT-nin Tähsil, Elm vä Mädäniyyät Täshkilatı
unexpected gözlanilmäz
unexploded bomb partlamamısh bomba
unfortunate bädbäkht
unfortunately bädbäkhtlikdän
unhappy qämli
UNHCR B.M.T.-nin Qachqınlar Üzrä Komisarlıghı
unification birläshdirmä; täshlikat; ittifaq
uniform uniforma, räsmi geyim
union ittifaq; *trade union* hämkarlar ittifaqı
unique täk
unite birläshmäk

United Nations Birläshmish Millätlär Täshkilatı
united birläshmish
university universitet
unknown namä'lum
unless -mäzsä/mazsa
until hälä ki
up yukharı
U.S.A. Amerika Birläshmish Shtatları (=A.B.Sh.)
use ishlätmä
useful faydalı
usual hämishäki
usually adätän

V

vacation mä'zunniyyät
vaccinated: I have been vaccinated. Män peyvänd olunmusham.
valley vadi
van furqon
variety qäläbä
varnish lak
vase vaza
vegetable shop täräväz dükanı
vegetables täräväz
vegetarian: I am a vegetarian. Män vegetarianam.
vein vena
venereal disease zöhrävi khastälik
verb fe'l
very chokh
veto veto; qadaghan
vice-president vitze-prezident
victim täläfat
victory qäläbä
video player videomaqnitofon; videopleyer
videotape cassette videokaset
view görkäm
village känd
village elder aghsakkal
vinegar sirkä
violence zorakılıq
virus virus
visa viza
visit *verb* görmäyä getmäk; *as a guest* qonaq getmäk
visitor gälän; *guest* qonaq
vodka aragh
voice säs
voltage regulator elektrik gärginliyin nizamlayıjısı
vomit: I have been vomiting. Män qusmusham.
vote *noun* säs
vote *verb* säs vermäk

vote-rigging säs vermänin saxtalashdırılması
voting säs vermä

W

wage war müharibä etmäk
wait gözlämäk
waiter ofisiant
waitress qadın ofisiant
wait for gözlämäk
wake oyatmaq; **Please wake me up at . . .** Zähmät olmasa, mäni saat . . . oyadin.
wake-up call oyatma zängi
Wales Vels
walkie-talkie äl radiosu
wall divar
wallet pul kisä
walnut qoz
want istämäk; **What do you want?; I want . . .** Män . . . istäyiräm.; **I don't want . . .** Män . . . istämiräm.
war müharibä; **civil war** vätandash müharibäsi
war crime härbi jinayät
war tribunal härbi tribunal
warm ilıgh
wash yumáq
wasp eshshäkarı
watch *noun* qol saatı
watch *verb* göz qoymaq; güdmäk
watchmaker's saatsaz dükanı
water su; **Is there drinking water?** Orada ichmäli su varmı?
water bottle su shüshäsi
waterfall shälalä
watermelon garpız
wave dalgha
way yol; **this way** bura(ya); **that way** ora(ya)
we biz
weak zäif
weapon silah
wear geymäk
weasel gälinjik
weather hava
Wednesday chärshänbä
week häftä; **last week** kechän häftä; **next week** gälän häftä; **this week** bu häftä
weekend häftä sonu; vikend
weep aghlamaq
weight chäki
welcome! *formal* Khosh gälmishsiniz!; *informal* Khosh gälmisän!
well *adjective* yakhshı
well *adverb* yakhshı

welcome!

well *noun* quyu; **oil well** neft quyusu;
gas well qaz quyusu
well site quyu qazima mä'däni
well-known mäshhur
Welsh velsli
west *noun* qärb
west(ern) *adjective* qärbi
wet *adjective* yash
wet *verb* islatmaq
what? nä?; **what kind?** nä?; **what's
that?** bu nädir?
wheat chovdar
wheel täkär
wheelchair täkärli oturajag
when? nä vakht?
where? harada?; **where from?**
haradan? **where is . . . ?**
. . . haradadır?; **where are . . . ?**
. . . haradadırlar?
which? hansı?
while ikän
whisky viski
white agh
who? kim?
whole bütün
why? niyä?
wide genish
widow dul qadın
widowed: **I am widowed.** Män
dulam.
widower dul kishi
wife arvad
wild vähshi
wild strawberry böyürtkän
win: **Who won?** Kim uddu?
wind *noun* küläk
wind *verb* qurmaq
window pänjärä
windshield qabaq shushä
windy küläkli
wine chakhir
wing qanad
winter qish
wire tel; mäftil
wisdom müdriklik
wish *verb* istämäk; **I wish to . . .** Män
istäyiräm . . .
with -la/-lä
withdraw geri chäkmäk
without -sız/-siz/-suz/-süz
witness shahid
wolf janavar
woman qadın
womb ushaqlıq
wood *forest* aghajlıq; *substance*
takhta
wool yun

work *noun* ish; **work/business trip**
e'zamiyyät
work *verb* ishlämäk; **The phone
doesn't work.** Telefon ishlämir.
worker ishchi
world dünya
worm qurd
worried: **to be worried** narahat
olmaq
worse chokh pis; **I feel worse.** Män
özümü chokh pis hiss ediräm.
worth däyär
wound *noun* yara
wound *verb* yaralamaq
wrapped bükülmüsh
wrench *noun*
wrestling güläsh
wrist äl
write yazmaq
writer yazıchı
writing yazı
writing paper y azmaq üchün kaghiz
wrong haqjız; **You're wrong!** Siz haqlı
deyilsiniz!

X

X-ray rentgen

Y

yard häyät; *distance* yard
year il; **last year** kechän il; **next year**
gälän il; **the year after next** gälän
ildän sonra; **this year** bu il
yellow sari
Yerevan Yerevan; *older form* İravan
yes bäli; hä *familiar*
yesterday dünän; **the day before
yesterday** sıragha gün
yet hälä; **not yet** hälä yokh
yield razılashmaq
yogurt qatıgh
you *plural* siz
you *singular* sän
young javan
young person gänj
your; yours *plural* sizin
your; yours *singular* sänin
yourself sän özün
yourselves siz özünüz

Z

zero sıfır
zoo zoopark

AZERBAIJANI
PHRASEBOOK

1. ETIQUETTE

Hello!	*familiar* **Salam!**
	formal **Salam äleyküm!**
How are you?	*familiar* **Nejäsän?**
	formal **Nejäsiniz?**
Fine, thank you.	**Sagh ol(un),* yakhshiyam.**
Good morning!	**Sabahin(ız)* kheyir!**
Good afternoon!	**Gunortan(ız)* kheyir!**
Good evening!	**Akhshamın(ız)* kheyir!**
Good night!	**Gejän(iz)* kheyrä qalsın!**
See you tomorrow!	**Sabah görüshänädäk!**
Good bye!	**Sag ol(un)!*/Khudahafiz!**
Bon voyage!	**Yolun(uz)* yüngül olsun!**
Welcome!	**Khosh gälmishsiniz (Khosh gälmisän)!***
Bon appetit!	**Nush olsun!**
Thank you	**Sag ol(un)!***
	Täshäkkür ediräm!
Good luck!	**Ughur olsun!**
Excuse me!	*familiar* **Baghıshlayın!**
	formal **Üzr istäyiräm!**
May I?	**Olarmı?**
Sorry!	*familiar* **Baghıshla!**
	formal **Üzr istäyiräm!**
yes**	**bäli;** *familiar* **hä**
no**	**yokh; kheyr**

Yä'ni . . . is a commonly heard expression meaning 'that is to say . . .' or 'I mean . . .'

* For formal expressions add ending in brackets. Use familiar forms when speaking to just one person who you know well or who's younger than you; use formal forms when speaking to more than one person, or to one person you don't know; or who is in a position of authority or respect, or significantly older than you.
** For more on 'yes' and 'no' see page 134.

2. QUICK REFERENCE

I	**män**
you *singular*	**sän**
he/she/it	**o**
we	**biz**
you *plural*	**siz**
they	**onlar**
this	**bu**
that	**o**
these	**bunlar**
those	**onlar**
here	**burada**
there	**orada**
where?	**harada?**
who?	**kim?**
what?	**nä?**
when?	**nä vakht?**
which?	**hansı?**
how?	**nejä?**
why?	**niyä?**
how far?	**nä qädär uzagh?**
how near?	**nä qädär yakhın?**
how much?	**nä qädär?**
how many?	**nechä dänä?**
what's that?	**bu nädir?**
is there?/are there?	**. . . oradadır(lar) mı?**
where is/are?	**. . . haradadır(lar)?**
what must I do?	**män nä etmäliyäm?**
what do you want?	*Familiar:* **Sän nä istäyirsän?**
	Formal: **Siz nä istäyirsiniz?**
very	**chokh**
and	**vä**
or	**vä ya; yakhud**
but	**lakin**
I like . . .	**. . . mänim khoshuma gälir.**

I don't like . . .	. . . mänim khoshuma gälmir.
I should like . . .	. . . mänim khoshuma gälmälidir.
I want . . .	Män . . . istäyiräm.
I don't want . . .	Män . . . istämiräm.
I know	Män . . . biliräm.
I don't know	Män . . . bilmiräm.
Do you understand?	*familiar* Sän basha düshdünmü?
	formal Siz anlayırsınızmı?
I understand.	Män anlayıram.
	Män basha düshüräm.
I don't understand.	Män basha düshmüräm.
	Män anlamıram.
I am sorry (to hear that).	Täässüflär olsun!
I am grateful.	Chokh minnätdaram.
It's important.	Bu chokh vajibdir.
It doesn't matter.	Bu vajib deyil.; Bir shey deyil.
You're welcome!	Buyurunuz!
No problem!	Problem deyil!
more or less	az-chokh
here is/here are	budur/bunlardır
Is everything OK?	Här shey yakhshıdırmı?
Danger!	Tählükä!
How do you spell that?	Bu söz necä säslänir?
I am . . .	
cold	mänä soyughdur
hot	mänä istidir
right	män yakhshıyam
sleepy	män yukhuluyam
hungry	män ajımısham
thirsty	män sustamısham
angry	mänä äsäbliyäm
happy	män khoshbäkhtäm
sad	män qämliyäm
tired	män yorghunam
well	män yakhshıyam

3. INTRODUCTIONS

What is your name?	**Adınız nädir?**
My name is . . .	**Adim . . .dir.**
May I introduce you to . . .	**Gälin sizi . . . la tanish edim.**
This is my . . .	**Bu mänim . . . -dir.***
friend.	**dostumdur.**
colleague/companion.	**hämkarimdir;**
	ish yoldashimdir.
relative.	**gohumumdur.**

TITLES – Mr., Mrs., Ms., and Miss are usually translated as follows: Mr. – **jänab** +surname, e.g. **Jänab Hill**; or first name + **bäy**, e.g. **Fred Bäy**. Miss/Ms./Mrs. – **khanım**, e.g. **Khanım Emma**, or **Emma Khanım**.

NATIONALITY

Where are you from?	**Siz haradansınız?**
I am from . . .	**Män . . .-danam.**
America	**Amerika**
Australia	**Avstraliya**
Britain	**Britaniya**
Canada	**Kanada**
England	**Ingiltärä****
Germany	**Almaniya**
Ireland	**Irlandiya**
New Zealand	**Yeni Zelandiya**
Northern Ireland	**Shimali Irlandiya**
Wales	**Vels**
Scotland	**Shotlandiya**
the USA	**Amerika Birläshmish Shtatları**** (=A.B.Sh.)
Europe	**Avropa**
India	**Hindistan**
Pakistan	**Pakistan**
Iran	**Iran**
Japan	**Yaponiya**

* or **-dır/-dür/-dur.**   ****-dänäm.**   *****-ndanam.**

I am . . .	**Män. . .**
American	**Amerikalıyam**
Australian	**Avstraliyalıyam**
British	**Britaniyalıyam**
Canadian	**Kanadalıyam**
Dutch	**Hollandiyalıyam**
English	**İngilisäm**
German	**Almanam**
Indian	**Hindäm**
Iranian	**İranliyam**
Irish	**İrlandiyalıyam**
Israeli	**İsraeliyam**
Pakistani	**Pakistanlıyam**
Welsh	**Velsliyam**
Scottish	**Shotlandam**

Where were you born?	**Siz harada anadan olmusuz?**
I was born in . . .	**Män . . . anadan olmusham.**

CAUCASIAN NATIONALITIES

Abkhaz	**Abkhaz**
Armenian	**Ermäni**
Avar	**Avar**
Azerbaijani	**Azärbayjanlı**
Georgian	**Gürjü**
Balkar	**Balkar**
Chechen	**Chechen**
Circassian	**Chärkäs**
Daghestani	**Daghıstanlı**
Ingush	**İngush**
Kabardian	**Kabardin**
Kalmuk	**Kalmık**
Karachai	**Karachay**
Kumyk	**Kumık**
Kurd	**Kürd**
Lezgi	**Läzgi**

Nogai	**Noqay**
Ossete	**Osetiyali**
Tat/Mountain Jew	**Tat**
Talysh	**Talış**

OCCUPATIONS

What do you do?	**Ishiniz nädir?**
I am a/an . . .	**Män . . .-am. (or -äm)**
academic	**elmi ishchi; elm adamı**
accountant	**muhasib**
administrator	**administrator**
agronomist	**aqronom**
aid worker	**humanitar täshkilatın ishchisi**
architect	**me'mar**
artist	**rässam**
business person	**ishküzar adam; biznesmen**
carpenter	**kharrat**
consultant	**mäslähätchi**
dentist	**dish häkimi**
diplomat	**diplomat**
doctor	**häkim**
economist	**iqtisadchı**
engineer	**mühändis**
farmer	**kändli; fermer**
filmmaker	**kino ishchisi**
journalist	**zhurnalist**
lawyer	**hüquqshunas; advokat**
mechanic	**mekhanik**
negotiator	**danishiqlari aparan shäkhs**
nurse	**tibb bajısı**
observer	**müshahidächi**
office worker	**ofis ishchisi**
pilot	**pilot**
political scientist	**politoloq**

scientist	**elmi ishchi;**
	researcher **tädqiqatchi**
secretary	*male* **katib;** *female* **katibä**
soldier	**äskär**
student	**täläbä**
surgeon	**järrah**
teacher	**müällim**
telecommunications	**televiziya ishchisi**
specialist	**mütäkhässis**
tourist	**turist**
writer	**yazıchı**

AGE

| How old are you? | **Nechä yashın(ız*) var?** |
| I am . . . years old. | **Mänim . . . yashım var.** |

FAMILY

Are you married?	**Evlisinizmi?**
I am single	**Män subayam.**
I am married.	*male* **Män evliyäm.**
	female **Män ärdäyäm.**
I am divorced.	**Män boshanmısham.**
I am widowed.	**Män dulam.**

Do you have a boyfriend?	**Siz bir oghlanla gäzirsinizmi?**
Do you have a girlfriend?	**Sizin qız dostunuz varmı?**
What is his/her name?	**Onun adı nädir?**
How many children do you have?	**Nechä ushaghınız var?**
I don't have any children.	**Mänim ushaghım yokhdur.**
I have a daughter.	**Mänim bir qızım var.**
I have a son.	**Mänim bir oghlum var.**
How many sisters do you have?	**Sizin nechä bajınız var?**
How many brothers do you have?	**Nechä qardashınız var?**

father	**ata**
mother	**ana**
grandfather	**baba**
grandmother	**nänä**
brother	**qardash**
sister	**baji**
children	**ushaghlar**
daughter	**qız**
son	**oghul**
twins	**äkizlär**
husband	**är**
wife	**arvad**
family	**ailä**
man	**kishi**
woman	**arvad**
boy	**oghlan**
girl	**qız**
person	**shäkhs**
people	**insanlar; adamlar**

RELIGION

The Azerbaijanis are a mostly Shi'i Muslim people. (For more, see the note on 'Religious Heritage' on page 127).

What is your religion?	**Dininiz nädir?; Siz hansı dinä mänsubsunuz?**
I am (a) . . .	**Män . . .-am**
Muslim	**müsälman**
Buddhist	**buddist; budda dindarı**
Orthodox	**pravoslav khristian**
Christian	**khristian; khachpäräst**
Catholic	**katolik**
Hindu	**hindu dindarı**
Jewish	**yahudi**

I am not religious. **Män dindar deyiläm.**

4. LANGUAGE

Aside from other indigenous languages spoken in the Caucasus, almost everyone in Azerbaijan speaks Russian. Many will also know a smattering at least of one or more European languages — such as German and English, while the older generations tend to know French. Because Azerbaijanis are found living over a wide area outside of the republic of Azerbaijan — added to which is the obvious influence of traditional Islam and modern politics — you will find many speakers of Farsi, Arabic and Turkish.

Do you speak English?	**Siz İngilisjä danıshırsınızmı?**
Do you speak Russian?	**Siz Ruscha danıshırsınızmı?**
Do you speak German?	**Siz Almanja danıshırsınızmı?**
Do you speak French?	**Siz Fransızja danıshırsınızmı?**
Do you speak Farsi?	**Siz Farscha danıshırsınızmı?**

Does anyone speak English?	**İngilisjä danıshan varmı?**
I speak a little . . .	**Män bir az . . . danıshıram.**
I don't speak . . .	**Män . . . danıshmıram.**
I understand.	**Män basha düshüräm.**
I don't understand.	**Män basha düshmüräm.**

Please point to the word in the book	**Zähmät olmasa, bu sözü kitabdan görsädin.**
Please wait while I look up the word	**Bir däqiqä gözläyin, lazımi sözü tapım.**
Could you speak more slowly, please?	**Khahish ediräm, bir az yavash danıshasınız.**
Could you repeat that?	**Täkrar edä bilärdinizmi?**
How do you say . . . in Azerbaijani?	**Azärbayjanja . . . nejä deyirsiz?**
What does . . . mean?	**. . . mä'nası nädir?**
How do you pronounce this word?	**Bu sözü nejä deyirsiz?**

I speak . . .	**Män . . . danışıram.**
Arabic	**äräbjä**
Armenian	**ermänijä**
Azeri	**azärbayjanja**
Chinese	**chin dilindä**
Danish	**danimarka dilindä**
Dutch	**holland dilindä**
English	**ingilisjä**
Farsi	**farscha**
French	**fransizja**
Georgian	**gürjü dilindä**
German	**almanja**
Greek	**yunanja**
Italian	**italyanja**
Japanese	**yaponja**
Ossete	**osetin dilindä**
Ukrainian	**ukrayna dilindä**
Russian	**ruscha**
Spanish	**ispanja**
Turkish	**türkjä**

5. BUREAUCRACY

Note that many forms you encounter may be still written in Russian instead.

your name	**adınız**
your surname	**familiyanız**
your middle name	**atanızın adı**
your address	**ünvan; yashadıghınız yer**
date of birth	**tävällüd; anadan olan gün**
place of birth	**anadan olan yer**
nationality	**millät**
age	**yash**
sex:	**jinsiyyat:**
male	**kishi**
female	**qadın**
religion	**dini mänsubiyyät**
reason for travel:	**säfärin mäqsädi:**
business	**ishküzar säfär; biznes**
tourism	**turizm**
work	**ish; e'zamiyyät**
personal	**shäkhsi**
profession	**peshä**
marital status:	**ailä:**
single	**subay**
married	*male* **evli**
	female **ärdä**
divorced	**boshanmısh**
date	**tarikh**
date of arrival	**gälish tarikhi**
date of departure	**gedish tarikhi**
passport	**pasport**
passport number	**pasportun nömräsi**
visa	**viza**
currency	**pul; valyuta**

MINISTRIES

Ministry of Defense	**Müdafiä Nazirliyi**
Ministry of Agriculture	**Känd Täsärrufatı Nazirliyi**
Ministry of Home Affairs	**Dakhili İshlär Nazirliyi**
Ministry of Foreign Affairs	**Khariji İshlär Nazirliyi**
Ministry of Transport	**Näqliyyat Nazirliyi**
Ministry of Health	**Sähiyyä Nazirliyi**
Ministry of Education	**Tähsil Nazirliyi**
Ministry of Justice	**Ädliyyä Nazirliyi**

Is this the correct form?	**Bu düz formadırmi?**
What does this mean?	**Bunun mä'nasi nädir?**
Where is . . . 's office?	**. . . ofisi haradadır?**
Which floor is it on?	**O, hansı märtäbädädir?**
Does the lift work?	**Lift ishläyirmi?**
Is Mr/Ms . . . in?	**Jänab/Khanım . . . yerindädirmi?**

Please tell him/her that I am here.	**Zähmät olmasa ona chatdırın ki, män buradayam.**
I can't wait, I have an appointment.	**Män gözläyä bilmäräm, mänim bashqa görüshlärim dä var.**
Tell him/her that I was here.	**Ona deyin ki, män gälmishdim.**

6. TRAVEL

Public transport – Buses or trolley buses can often be too packed for comfort, and Baku's metro is being swiftly outpaced by the growth of new suburbs. Far more practical are the numerous privately run minibuses (locally called **mikro-avtobus**) which stop at predetermined pick-up points. You pay the driver's assistant when you get out. Longer distance travel out of town offers you the usual variety of means. There are now many car rental firms, offering you vehicles with or without drivers. Rates vary. Buses are reliable and leave from specially designated areas. Intercity buses usually wait to collect the most possible number of passengers. Travel by rail is slow and subject to long delays mid-journey. Note that all public announcements, particularly for trains and planes, are made both in Azerbaijani and Russian. Bicycles and motorbikes are not difficult to find and, in view of the bad roads in much of the country, are often a practical alternative. These are not used much in city areas, however.

What time does . . . leave/arrive?	**. . . nä zaman qalkhır/ gälir?**
the airplane	**täyyarä; uchaq**
the boat	**gämi**
the bus	**avtobus**
the train	**qatar**
the trolley bus	**troleybus**
The plane is delayed/ cancelled.	**Täyyarä gejikir/sakhlanılıb.**
The train is delayed/ cancelled.	**Gatar gejikir/sakhlanılıb.**
How long will it be delayed?	**Nä qädär gejikir?**
There is a delay of . . .	**Gejikmä zamanı . . .-dir.**
Excuse me, where is the ticket office?	**Baghıshlayın, bilet kassası haradadır?**
Where can I buy a ticket?	**Män bileti harada ala biläräm?**

I want to go to . . .	**Män . . . getmäk istäyiräm.**
I want a ticket to . . .	**Män . . . qädär bilet istäyiräm.**
I would like . . .	**Män . . . istäyiräm.**
a one-way ticket	**bir basha bilet**
a return ticket	**o bash bu basha bilet**
first class	**birinji klas**
second class	**ikinji klas**
business class	**biznes klas**
Do I pay in dollars or in manats?	**Män pulu dollar yokhsa manatla ödämäliyäm?**
You must pay in dollars.	**Siz pulu dollarla ödämälisiniz.**
You must pay in manats.	**Siz pulu manatla ödämälisiniz.**
You can pay in either.	**Här hansı pul ilä verä bilärsiniz.**
Can I reserve a place?	**Män yeri ävväljädän sifarish edä bilärämmi?**
How long does the trip take?	**Yolumuz nä qädär vakht aparajaq?**
Is it a direct route?	**Yolumuz düzdürmü?**

AIR

In Azerbaijan all flights are (technically) non-smoking.

Is there a flight to . . . ?	**. . . uchush varmı?**
When is the next flight to . . . ?	**. . . uchush nä zaman olajaq?**
How long is the flight?	**Uchushun müddäti nä qädärdir?**
What is the flight number?	**Uchushun nömräsi hansıdır?**
You must check in at . . .	**Siz qeydiyyatdan . . . kechmälisiniz.**
Is the flight delayed?	**Uchush gejikirmi?**
How many hours is the flight delayed?	**Uchush nechä saat gejikir?**
Is this the flight for . . . ?	**Bu . . . uchushudurmu?**
Is that the flight from . . . ?	**Bu . . .-dan gälän uchushdurmu?**
When is the Moscow flight arriving?	**Moskva uchushu (reysi) nä zaman gözlänilir?**

Is it on time?	**O, vakhtındamı gälir?**
Is it late?	**O, gejikirmi?**
Do I have to change planes?	**Män täyyäräläri däyishmäli olajaghammı?**
Has the plane left Moscow yet?	**Täyyärä Moskvadan chıkhıbmı?**
What time does the plane take off?	**Täyyärä nä zaman qalkhir?**
What time do we arrive in Moscow?	**Biz Moskvaya nä zaman enäjäyik?**
excess baggage	**artıgh baqazh**
international flight	**beynälkhalq uchush**
internal flight	**dakhili uchush**

BUS

bus stop	**avtobus dayanajaghı**
Where is the bus stop/ station?	**Avtobus dayanajaghı/ stansiyası haradadır?**
Take me to the bus station.	**Mäni avtobus stansiyasına apar.**
Which bus goes to . . . ?	**. . . hansı avtobus gedir?**
Does this bus go to . . . ?	**Bu avtobus . . . gedirmi?**
How often do buses pass by?	**Avtobuslar tezmi kechirlär?**
What time is the . . . bus?	**. . . avtobus nä zaman olajaq.**
next	**növbäti**
first	**birinji**
last	**akhırınjı; sonunju**
Will you let me know when we get to . . . ?	**. . . chatanda, mänä khäbär verärsinizmi?**
Stop, I want to get off!	**Sakhla, düshmäk istäyiräm!**
Where can I get a bus to . . . ?	**Män . . . gedän avtobusa harada minä biläräm?**
When is the first bus to . . . ?	**. . . birinji avtobus nä vakht qalkhır?**

When is the last bus to ... ?	... akhırınjı (son) avt· vakht qalkhır?
When is the next bus to ... ?	... növbäti avtobus nä vakht (zaman) qalkhır?
Do I have to change buses?	**Män avtobusları däyishmäliyämmi?**

I want to get off at ...	**Män ... düshmäk istäyiräm.**
Please let me off at the next stop.	**Zähmät olmasa, növbäti dayanajaghda imkan verin düshüm.**
Please let me off here.	**Zähmät olmasa, burada sakhlayin düshüm.**
How long is the journey?	**Säfärin müddäti nä qädärdir?**
What is the fare?	**Yol pulu nä qädärdir?**
I need my luggage, please.	**Mänim baqazhımı verin, zähmät olmasa.**
That's my bag.	**Bu chanta mänimdir.**

RAIL

Passengers must ...	**Särnishinlär ...**
change trains.	**qatarları däyishmälidirlär.**
change platforms.	**platformaları däyishmälidirlär.**
Is this the right platform for ... ?	**... -ya gedän qatar üchün düz platformadırmı?**
The train leaves from platform ...	**Qatar ... platformadan yola düshür.**
Is there a timetable?	**Jädväl varmı?**
Take me to the railway station.	**Mäni qatar stansiyasına apar.**
Which platform should I go to?	**Män hansı platformaya getmäliyäm?**
platform one/two	**birinji/ikinji platformaya**
You must change trains at ...	**Siz qatarları ... däyishmälisiniz.**

Where can I buy tickets?	**Män biletläri haradan ala biläräm?**
Will the train leave on time?	**Qatar vakhtiındamı yola düshür?**
There will be a delay of . . . minutes.	**Qatar . . . däqiqä gej olajaq.**
There will be a delay of . . . hours.	**Qatar . . . saat gej olajaq.**

TAXI

Some taxis are marked , while others are not. You can also wave down and negotiate a fare with any private car willing to go your way, although this is not always as safe. To avoid unpleasant surprises, agree to fares in advance. It is useful to be able to tell the driver your destination in Azerbaijani or Russian (or have it written down on a piece of paper). Be warned, however, that some drivers will have as little idea as you as to the precise whereabouts of your destination. A reliable option is to call up one of the growing number of radio taxi companies.

Taxi!	**Taksi!**
Where can I get a taxi?	**Taksi harada sakhlayir?**
Please could you get me a taxi.	**Zähmät olmasa, mänä taksi sakhlayın.**
Can you take me to . . . ?	**Mäni . . . apararsınmı?**
Please take me to . . .	**Zähmät olmasa mäni . . . aparın.**
How much will it cost to . . . ?	**Haqqı nä olajagh?**
To this address, please.	**Bu ünvana, zähmät olmasa.**
Turn left.	**Sola dön.**
Turn right.	**Sagha dön.**
Go straight ahead.	**Düz sür.**
Stop!	**Sakhla!**
Don't stop!	**Sakhlama!**
I'm in a hurry.	**Män täläsiräm.**
Please drive more slowly!	**Bir az yavash sür!**
Here is fine, thank you.	**Burda sakhla, sagh ol.**

The next corner, please.	**O biri tindä sakhla.**
The next street to the left.	**Növbäti küchädä sola dön.**
The next street to the right.	**Növbäti küchädä sagha dön.**
Stop here!	**Burada sakhla!**
Stop the car, I want to get out.	**Mashını sakhla, män düshüräm.**
Please wait here.	**Burada gözlä.**
Take me to the airport.	**Mäni aeroporta apar.**

GENERAL PHRASES

I want to get off at . . .	**Män . . . düshmäk istäyiräm.**
Excuse me!	**Baghıshlayın! Üzr istäyiräm!**
Excuse me, may I get by?	**Baghıshlayın, kechmäk olarmı?**
These are my bags.	**Bu mänim chantalarımdır.**
Please put them there.	**Zähmät olmasa oları bura qoyun.**
Is this seat free?	**Bu oturajaq boshdurmu?**
I think that's my seat.	**Mänjä, bu mänim yerimdir.**

EXTRA WORDS

airport	**aeroport; hava limanı**
airport tax	**aeroport vergisi**
ambulance	**täjili yardım**
arrivals	**qälish**
baggage counter	**baqazh bölmäsi**
bicycle	**velosiped**
boarding pass	**täyyaräyä kechid burakhılıshı**
boat	**gämi**
bus stop	**avtobus dayanajaghı**
car	**mashin; avtomobil**
check-in counter	**qeydiyyat bölmäsi**
check-in	**qeydiyyat**
closed	**baghlı**
customs	**gömrük**
delay	**gejikmä**
departures	**uchushlar**

dining car	**vaqon-restoran**
emergency exit	**avariya chıkhıshı**
entrance	**girish**
exit	**chıkhısh**
express	**ekspres**
ferry	**bärä**
4-wheel drive	**jip**
information	**mä'lumat**
ladies/gents	**qadın/kishi tualeti; ayaqyolu**
local	**yerli**
helicopter	**helikopter**
horse and cart	**at arabası**
motorbike	**motosiklet**
no entry	**girish qadaghandir**
no smoking	**sigaret chäkmäk qadaghandır**
open	**achıq**
platform number	**platforma nömräsi**
railway	**dämir yolu**
reserved	**sifarish edilib**
radio taxi	**radiolu taksi**
road	**yol**
sign	**isharä**
sleeping car	**yataq vaqonu**
station	**stansiya**
subway	**yeraltı kechid**
telephone	**telefon**
ticket office	**bilet kassası**
timetable	**jädväl**
toilet(s)	**tualet; ayaghyolu**
town center	**shähär märkäzi**
train station	**dämir yolu stansiyası**
trolley bus	**troleybus**

7. ACCOMMODATION

Aside from the main hotels, which are mostly in Baku and provide service to US/European standards, you will find that room service is not always available, and breakfast or other meals will have to be negotiated and paid for separately. An excellent option in more rural areas is to have your accommodation arranged at a private house, where traditional hospitality will guarantee that you are well looked after and — as always in Azerbaijan — well fed.

I am looking for a . . .	**Män . . . akhtariram.**
guesthouse	**qonaq evi**
hotel	**mehmankhana; otel**
hostel	**yataqkhana**
Is there anywhere I can stay for the night?	**Burda gejälämäyä yer varmı?**
Is there anywhere we can stay for the night?	**Bizimchun gejäni qalmagha yer varmı?**
Where is . . . ?	**. . . hardadır?**
a cheap hotel	**ujuz mehmankhana**
a good hotel	**yakhshi mehmankhana**
a nearby hotel	**yakhında yerläshän mehmankhana**
a clean hotel	**tämiz mehmankhana**
What is the address?	**Ünvanı nädir?**
Could you write the address please?	**Ünvanı mänim üchün yaza bilärsinizmi?**

AT THE HOTEL

Do you have any rooms free?	**Sizdä bosh otaqlar varmı?**
I would like . . .	**Män . . . istärdim.**
a single room	**täk otaq**
a double room	**ikinäfärlik otaq**
We'd like a room.	**Biz bir otaq istäyirik.**
We'd like two rooms.	**Biz iki otaq istäyirik.**

I want a room with . . .	**Män istäyiräm otaghımda . . . olsun.**
a bathroom	**hamam; vanna otaghı**
a shower	**dush**
a television	**televizor**
a window	**penjärä**
a double bed	**ikiliy yataq**
a balcony	**eyvan; balkon**
a view	**görkäm**
I want a room that's quiet.	**Män sakit bir otaq istäyiräm.**
How long will you be staying?	**Siz hansı müddätä qalajaghsınız?**
How many nights?	**Nechä gejä?**
I'm going to stay for . . .	**Män . . . qalajam.**
one day	**bir gün**
two days	**iki gün**
one week	**bir häftä**
Do you have any I.D.?	**Sizdä här hansı bir sänäd varmı?**
Sorry, we're full.	**Baghishlayın, bosh otaghımız yokhdur.**
I have a reservation.	**Mänim otaghım sifarish olunub.**
My name is . . .	**Mänim adım . . .**
May I speak to the manager please?	**Män räisinizlä/administratorla danısha bilirämmi?**
I have to meet someone here.	**Män bir adamla burada qörüshmäliyäm.**
How much is it per night/ per person?	**Bir adama gejäsi nechäyädir?**
How much is it per week?	**Häftäsi nechäyädir?**
It's . . . per day/per person.	**Bir adama bir günü . . .**
Can I see it?	**Män onu görä bilärämmi?**
Are there any others?	**Bashqaları varmı?**
Is there . . . ?	**Orada . . . varmı?**
air-conditioning	**kondisioner**
a telephone	**telefon**

hot water	**isti su**
laundry service	**paltarın yuyulması khidmäti**
room service	**otaghı tämizlämä khidmäti**
No, I don't like it.	**Yokh, bu mänim khoshuma gälmir**
It's too . . .	**Bu hättindän artıq . . .**
cold	**soyuq**
hot	**isti**
big	**böyük**
dark	**qaranlıq**
small	**balaja**
noisy	**säs-küylü**
dirty	**chirkli**
It's fine, I'll take it.	**Yakhshıdır, män bunu götürüräm.**
Where is the bathroom?	**Hamam haradadır?**
Is there hot water all day?	**Isti su bütün günmü gälir?**
Do you have a safe?	**Sizdä seyf varmı?**
Is there anywhere to wash clothes?	**Burada harada paltar yumaq olar?**
Can I use the telephone?	**Telefondan istifadä edä bilärämmi?**

NEEDS

I need . . .	**Mänä . . . lazımdır.**
candles	**shamlar**
toilet paper	**tualet kaghızı**
soap	**sabun**
clean sheets	**tämiz mäläfä**
an extra blanket	**älavä yorghan**
drinking water	**ichmäli su**
a lightbulb	**lampa**
Please change the sheets.	**Zähmät olmasa, örtäyi däyishin.**

I can't open/close the window.	**Män pänjäräni acha/baghlaya bilmiräm.**
I have lost my key.	**Män otaghıımın acharını itirmishäm.**
Can I have the key to my room?	**Otaghımın acharını ala bilirämmi?**
The toilet won't flush.	**Tualet ishlämir.**
The water has been cut off.	**Suyu käsilib.**
The electricity has been cut off.	**Ishıq käsilib.**
The gas has been cut off.	**Qaz käsilib.**
The heating has been cut off.	**Isitmä käsilib.**
The heater doesn't work.	**Isitmä qazanı ishlämir.**
The air-conditioning doesn't work.	**Kondisioner ishlämir.**
The phone doesn't work.	**Telefon ishlämir.**
I can't flush the toilet.	**Tualetin suyunu chäkä bilmiräm.**
The toilet is blocked.	**Tualetin borusu tutulub.**
I can't switch off the tap.	**Män su kranını (lüläyini) baghlaya bilmiräm.**
I need a plug for the bath.	**Mänä vanna üchün tıkhaj lazımdır.**
Where is the plug socket?	**Elektrik rozeti haradadır?**
wake-up call	**oyatma zängi**
Could you please wake me up at . . . o'clock.	**Zähmät olmasa mäni saat . . . oyadın.**
I am leaving now.	**Män indi gediräm.**
We are leaving now.	**Biz indi gedirik.**
May I pay the bill now?	**Hesabımı indi ödäyä bilirämmi?**

EXTRA WORDS

bathroom	**hamam; vanna otagı**
bed	**yataq**

blanket	**yorghan**
candle	**sham**
chair	**kreslo; qoltuqlu kürsü**
cold water	**soyuq su**
cupboard	**dolab; shkaf; shifoner**
doorlock	**kilid**
electricity	**ishıq; elektrik**
excluded	**kharij olaraq (kharij edilmish)**
fridge	**soyuduju**
hot water	**isti su**
included	**dakhil olmaqla; dakhil edilmish**
key	**achar**
laundry	**yuyulajaq paltar**
mattress	**döshäk**
meals	**yemäklär**
mirror	**güzgü**
name	**ad**
noisy	**säs-küylü**
padlock	**qıfıl**
pillow	**bashaltı**
plug (bath)	**tıkhaj**
plug (electric)	**rozetka**
quiet	**sakit**
room	**otaq**
room number	**otaghın nömräsi**
sheet	**mäläfä**
shower	**dush**
suitcase	**chamadan**
surname	**familiya**
table	**masa**
towel	**däsmal**
water	**su**
window	**pänjärä**

8. FOOD AND DRINK

Food plays an important part of Azerbaijani life, and key events in all aspects of life and the seasons are marked with a feast of one form or another. Expect to be offered a dazzling variety of dishes, delicacies and drinks, which vary from region to region and from season to season.

breakfast	**sähär yemäyi**
lunch	**nahar**
snack	**galyanaltı**
dinner/supper	**sham/akhsham yemäyi**
dessert	**desert; chäräz**

I'm hungry.	**Män ajımısham.**
I'm thirsty.	**Män sustamisham.**
Do you know a good restaurant?	**Yakhshı restoran yeri bilirsinizmi?**
Do you have a table, please?	**Bosh masanız varmı?**
I would like a table for . . . people, please.	**Zähmät olmasa, bizä . . .- näfärlik masa täshkil edin.**
Can I see the menu please?	**Menyuya bakha bilärämmi?**
I'm still looking at the menu.	**Män hälälik menyuya bakhıram.**
I would like to order now.	**Män indi sifarish veräjäyäm.**
What's this?	**Bu nädir?**
Is it spicy?	**Bu istiotludurmu?**
Does it have meat in it?	**Bu yemäkdä ät varmı?**
Does it have alcohol in it?	**Bu alkoholludurmu?**
Do you have . . . ?	**Sizdä . . . varmı?**
We don't have . . .	**Bizdä . . . yokhdur.**
What would you recommend?	**Siz näyi mäslähät görärdiniz?**
Do you want . . . ?	**Siz . . . istäyirsinizmi?**
Can I order some more . . . ?	**Män bir az da . . . sifarish edä bilärämmi?**

That's all, thank you.	**Bu qädär, sagh olun.**
That's enough, thanks.	**Bu qädär bästir, sagh olun.**
I haven't finished yet.	**Män hälä bitirmämishäm.**
I have finished eating.	**Män yemäyi qurtarmısham.**
I am full up!	**Män doymusham.**
Where are the toilets?	**Tualetiniz haradadır?**

I am a vegetarian.	**Män vegetarianam.**
I don't eat meat.	**Män ät yemiräm.**
I don't eat pork.	**Män donuz äti yemiräm.**
I don't eat chicken or fish.	**Män toyuq vä ya balıg yemiräm.**
I don't drink alcohol.	**Män alkohol ichmiräm.**
I don't smoke.	**Män sigaret chäkmiräm.**

I would like . . .	**Zähmät olmasa, mänä . . . gätirin.**
an ashtray	**külgabı**
the bill	**hesab**
a glass of water	**bir stäkan su**
a bottle of water	**bir shüshä su**
a bottle of wine	**bir shüshä chakhir**
a bottle of beer	**bir shüshä pivä**
another bottle	**bir dänä dä shüshä**
a bottle opener	**shüshä achan**
a corkscrew	**burghu; probka achan**
dessert	**chäräz; desert**
a drink	**ichki**
a fork	**chängäl**
another chair	**älavä oturajaq**
another plate	**älavä boshqab**
another glass	**älavä stäkan**
another cup	**älavä dolcha**
a napkin	**älsilän; khoräk däsmalı**
a glass	**stäkan;** *small* **shots gädäh**
a knife	**bıchaq**

a plate	**boshqab**
a samovar	**samovar**
a spoon	**qashıq**
a table	**masa**
a teaspoon	**chay qashığı**
a toothpick	**dish üchün chöp**

fresh	**täzä**
spicy (hot)	**istiotlu**
stale	**köhnä; bayat**
sour	**kämshirin**
sweet	**shirin**
bitter	**ajı**
hot	**isti**
cold	**soyuq**
salty	**duzlu**
tasteless	**dadsız**
bad	**pis**
tasty	**dadlı**
too much	**häddindän artıgh chokh**
too little	**häddindän artıgh az**
not enough	**kifayät deyil; qeyri-kafi**

FOOD

bread	**chöräk**
candy	**shirniyyat**
caviar	**kürü**
cheese	**pendir**
chewing gum	**saqqız**
egg	**yumurta**
flour	**khämir**
french fries	**qızardılmısh kartof**
hamburger	**hamburger**
honey	**bal**
ice cream	**dondurma**
ketchup	**ketchup**

mustard	**khardal**
nut	**qoz**
oil	**yagh**
pasta	**khämir yemäyi (garniri)**
pepper	**istiot**
pizza	**pitsa**
rice	**düyi**
salad	**salat**
salt	**duz**
sandwich	**buterbrod**
soup	**shorba; sup**
sugar	**qänd**
vinegar	**sirkä**
yoghurt	**qatıgh**

VEGETABLES

beetroot	**chughundur**
cucumber	**khiyar**
potato	**kartof**
pepper	**istiot**
tomato	**pamidor**
vegetables	**täräväz**

FRUIT

apple	**alma**
grape	**üzüm**
lemon	**lumu**
melon	**yemish**
orange	**portaghal**
peach	**shaftalı**
plum	**gavalı**
sour plum	**alcha**
strawberry	**chiyäläk**
wild strawberry	**böyürtkän**
watermelon	**qarpız**

MEAT

beef	**mal äti**
chicken	**toyuq**
fish	**balıq**
kebab	**käbab**
lamb	**quzu**
pork	**donuz**
sausage	**kolbasa**

DRINKS

Remember to ask for modern soft drinks by brand name.

alcohol	**alkohol**
beer	**pivä**
bottle	**shüshä**
brandy	**brendi;** *Soviet varieties are called* **konyak**
can	**banka**
champagne	**shampan**
coffee	**qähvä**
coffee with milk	**südlü qähvä**
cognac	**konyak**
fruit juice	**meyvä suyu**
ice	**buz**
milk	**süd**
mineral water	**mineral su**
tea	**chay**
tea with lemon	**lumulu chay**
tea with milk	**südlü chay**
no sugar, please	**shäkärsiz, zähmät olmasa**
vodka	**aragh**
whisky	**viski**
wine	**chakhır**
red	**qırmızı**
sparkling	**qazlı**
white	**agh**

MORE ON FOOD AND DRINK

Food in Azerbaijan is a great discovery for the visitor. Each part of Azerbaijan has its unique cuisine with its own special flavor. There is a wide variety of meat, fowl or fish based stews and grills, surrounded with nuts and vegetables and garnished with coriander, mint, pepper and basil. Some common specialities include:

> **dolma** — lamb mince with herbs and rice, wrapped in vine leaves (**yarpaq doması**) or cabbage (**käläm dolması**).
>
> **lülä käbab** — kebab made with minced lamb.
>
> **tikä käbab** — kebab made with chunks of lamb meat grilled on charcoal.
>
> **antrekot** — kebab made of lamb ribs.
>
> **lävängi** — oven-cooked chicken stuffed with walnuts, herbs and nuts.
>
> **düshbärä** — small, compact dumpling stuffed with mince, served piping hot with yoghurt and herbs.
>
> **qutab** — like a large pitta bread, but thinner and stuffed with meat or herbs.

Accompanying the above will be seasonal salads and sauces – best when home-made. Finish off your meal with fruit, all washed down with the ubiquitous tea or mineral water bottled from one of the country's many natural sources.

Alcohol – Alcohol is drunk everywhere, as in other parts of the Caucasus. You may encounter disapproval in some cases for religious reasons, which should be respected.

Azerbaijanis have developed a finely tuned tradition of feasting in the form of the **mäjlis**, or banquet, Course after course is brought to a long table around which the diners sit. The only essential phrases to know here: **Sagh ol!** or **Deyilän saghligha!** – 'Cheers!'

9. DIRECTIONS

Where is . . . ?	. . . haradadır?
the academy	akademiya
the airport	aeroport; hava limanı
the art gallery	injäsänät qalereyası
a bank	bank
the cathedral	kirkha
the church	kilsä
the city center	shähär märkäzi
the consulate	konsulluq
the . . . embassy	. . . säfirliyi
my hotel	mänim mehmankhanam
the information office	mälumat bürosu
the main square	bash meydan
the market	bazar
the Ministry of . . .	. . . nazirliyi
the monastery	monastır
the mosque	mäschid
the museum	muzey
parliament	parlament
Azerbaijani parliament	Milli Mäjlis
the police station	polis shö'bäsi
the post office	pocht
the station	stansiya
the synagogue	sinaqoq
the telephone center	telefon danıshıqları märkäzi
a toilet	tualet; ayaghyolu
the university	universitet

What . . . is this?	Bu . . . nädir?
bridge	körpü
building	bina
district	rayon; ärazi
river	chay

road	**yol**
street	**küchä**
suburb	**shähärätrafı qäsäbä**
town	**shähär**
village	**känd**

What is this building?	**Bu binada nä yerläshir?**
What is that building?	**O binada nä yerläshir?**
What time does it open?	**O nä zaman achılır?**
What time does it close?	**O nä zaman baghlanır?**

Can I park here?	**Män mashını burada sakhlaya bilärämmi?**

Are we on the right road for . . . ?	**Bu yol . . . aparırmı?**
How many kilometers is it to . . . ?	**. . . qädär nechä kilometrdir?**
It is . . . kilometers away.	**O . . . kilometr mäsafädädir.**
How far is the next village?	**Növbäti känd uzaqdırmı?**

Where can I find this address?	**Bu ünvan haradadır?**
Can you show me on the map?	**Khäritädä göstärä bilärsinizmi?**
How do I get to . . . ?	**Män . . . nejä gedä biläräm?**
I want to go to . . .	**Män . . . getmäk istäyiräm.**
Can I walk there?	**Män oraya piyada gedä bilärämmi?**

Is it far?	**O uzaqdırmı?**
Is it near?	**O yakhindırmı?**
Is it far from/near here?	**O buradan uzaqdırmı/ yakhındırmı?**

It is not far.	**O uzaq deyil.**

DIRECTIONS

Go straight ahead.	**Düz gedin.**
It's two blocks down.	**O iki kvartal ashaghıdır**
Turn left.	**Sola dön.**
Turn right.	**Sagha dön.**
at the next corner	**növbäti tindä**
at the traffic lights	**svetoforda/ishıqforda**
behind	**arkhada**
far	**uzaqda**
in front of	**qabaghında**
left	**sol**
near	**yakhın**
opposite	**üzbäüz; äksinä**
right	**sagh**
straight on	**düz qabagha**
bridge	**körpü**
corner	**tin**
crossroads	**tinbashı; dörd yol aghzı**
one-way street	**birtäräfli häräkat küchäsi**
north	**shimal**
south	**jänub**
east	**shärq**
west	**qärb**

10. SHOPPING

Where can I find a . . . ?	**Män . . . harada tapa biläräm?**
Where can I buy . . . ?	**Män . . . harada ala biläräm?**
Where's the market?	**Bazar haradadır?**
Where's the nearest . . . ?	**Än yakhın . . . haradadır?**
Can you help me?	**Mänä kömäk edä bilärsinizmi?**
Can I help you?	**Sizä kömäk lazımdırmı?**
I'm just looking.	**Sadäjä bakhıram.**
I'd like to buy . . .	**Män . . . almaq istärdim.**
Could you show me some . . . ?	**Siz mänä . . . göstärä bilärdinizmi?**
Can I look at it?	**Män buna bakha bilärämmi?**
Do you have any . . . ?	**Sizdä här hansı . . . varmı?**
This.	**Bu.**
That.	**O.**
I don't like it.	**Bu mänim khoshuma gälmir.**
I like it.	**Bu mänim khoshuma gälir.**
Do you have anything cheaper?	**Sizdä bundan daha ujuz här hansı bir shey varmı?**
cheaper/better	**daha ujuz/daha yakhshı**
larger/smaller	**daha böyük/balaja**
Do you have anything else?	**Sizdä bashqa bir shey varmı?**
Do you have any others?	**Sizdä bashqalarindan varmı?**
Sorry, this is the only one.	**Täässüf ki, täk bu qalib.**
I'll take it.	**Män bunu götürüräm.**
How much/many do you want?	**Siz nä qädär/nechä dänä istäyirsiniz?**
How much is it?	**Bu nechäyädir?**
Can you write down the price?	**Qiymäti yazarsınızmı?**
Could you lower the price?	**Qiymäti bir az ashaghı salmaq mümkündürmü?**

I don't have much money.	**Mänim o qädär pulum yokhdur.**
Do you take credit cards?	**Siz kredit kartını qäbul edirsinizmi?**
Would you like it wrapped?	**Bunu sizin üchün bükäkmi?**
Will that be all?	**Bunlarla bitirmi?**
Thank you, goodbye.	**Täshäkkürlär, sagh olun.**
I want to return this.	**Män bunu qaytarmaq istäyiräm.**

OUTLETS

auto supply shop	**ehtiyat hissäläri maghazası**
baker's	**chöräk maghazası**
bank	**bank**
barber's	**bärbärkhana; dälläkkhana**
I'd like a haircut, please.	**Bashımı vurdurmaq istäyiräm.**
bookshop	**kitab maghazası**
butcher's	**ät dükanı**
pharmacy	**äjzachıkhana; aptek**
clothes shop	**paltar dükanı**
dairy	**süd maghazası**
dentist	**dish häkimi**
department store	**univermaq**
dressmaker	**paltarkäsän; därzi**
electrical goods store	**elektrik jıhazlar maghazası**
florist	**gül dükanı**
greengrocer	**göyärtisatan; säbzävatchi**
hairdresser	**bärbär; dälläk**
hardware store	**täsärrufat malları dükanı**
hospital	**khästäkhana**
kiosk	**kiosk**
laundry	**paltaryuyan; paltartämizläyän**
market	**bazar**
newsstand	**qäzet dükanı**

shoeshop	**ayaqqabi dükanı**
shop	**dükan; maghaza**
souvenir shop	**suvenir dükanı; hädiyyälär maghazası**
stationer's	**däftärkhana malları maghazası**
supermarket	**univermaq; supermarket**
travel agent	**turist agentliyi**
vegetable shop	**tärävaz dükanı**
watchmaker's	**saatsaz dükanı**

GIFTS

Arts & Crafts – Azerbaijan boasts numerous artists of varying quality and there are a number of antique shops notably in Baku's **I chäri Shähär** ('Inner Castle'). Remember that there are restrictions on what you can take out of the country. Buying art is little problem as every Azerbaijani seems to have a friend who is an artist or craftsman. So you can spend many a pleasant afternoon as you are taken round various houses to examine mini collections. Quality art is also sold in the street and parks, e.g. metal work, jewelry and wood carvings. The best places still to buy gifts and souvenirs are the 'salons,' the official handicrafts galleries.

Antiquities – Remember that it is illegal to take out of the country any Azerbaijani antiquities unless accompanied by the relevant paperwork.

box	**yeshik**
bracelet	**qolbagh**
brooch	**brosh**
candlestick	**shamdan**
carpet	**khalcha**
chain	**zänjir**
clock	**saat**
copper	**mis**
crystal	**büllur; kristal**
earrings	**sırghalar**
enamel	**mina**
gold	**qızıl**

handicraft	**äl ishi**
iron	**polad**
jade	**dash**
jewelry	**zärgärlik malları**
kilim	**kilim**
leather	**däri**
metal	**metal**
modern	**müasir**
necklace	**boyunbaghı; hämail**
pottery	**duluschu äshyaları**
ring	**üzük**
rosary	**täsbäy**
silver	**gümüsh**
steel	**polad**
stone	**dash; qash**
traditional	**än'änävi**
vase	**vaza**
watch	**qol saat**
wood	**aghaj**

CLOTHES

bag	**chanta**
belt	**kämär**
boots	**chäkmälär**
cotton	**pambıgh**
dress	**paltar; don**
gloves	**äljäk**
handbag	**äl chantası**
hat	**papagh**
jacket	**penjäk**
jeans	**jins**
leather	**däri**
necktie	**qalstuk**
overcoat	**palto; kürk**
pocket	**jib**
scarf	**shärf**

shirt	**köynäk**
shoes	**tufli**
socks	**jorablar**
suit	**kostyum**
sweater	**sviter; yun köynäk**
tights	**qadın jorabları**
trousers	**shalvar**
umbrella	**chätir**
underwear	**alt paltar**
uniform	**uniforma; räsmi geyim**
wool	**yun**

TOILETRIES

aspirin	**aspirin**
Band-Aid	**plastır**
comb	**daragh**
condom	**prezervativ**
cotton wool	**pambıgh**
deodorant	**deodorant**
hairbrush	**daragh**
lipstick	**dodaq pomadası**
mascara	**sürmä**
mouthwash	**aghız üchün qar-qara därmanı**
nail-clippers	**dırnaq qaychısı**
painkillers	**aghrıkäsän därmanlar**
perfume	**ätir**
powder	**toz**
razor	**üzqırkhma jıhazı**
razorblade	**üzqırkhma ülgüjü**
safety pin	**sanjaq**
shampoo	**shampun**
shaving cream	**üzqırkhma kremi**
sleeping pills	**yokhu därmanı**
soap	**sabun**
sponge	**lif**
sunblock cream	**günäsh shualarına qarshı krem**

tampons	**tıkhaj; piltä; tampon**
thermometer	**termometr**
tissues	**däsmallar**
toilet paper	**tualet kaghızı**
toothbrush	**dish shotkası**
toothpaste	**dish pastası**

STATIONERY

ballpoint	**diyirjäkli qäläm**
book	**kitab**
dictionary	**sözlük**
envelope	**zärf**
guidebook	**turist kitabchası**
ink	**müräkkäb**
magazine	**därgi; zhurnal**
map	**khäritä**
road map	**yol khäritäsi; yol atlası**
a map of Baku	**Bakının khäritäsi**
newspaper	**qäzet**
newspaper in English	**İngilisjä qäzet**
notebook	**kitabcha**
novels in English	**İngilisjä romanlar**
(piece of) paper	**(bir parcha) kaghız**
pen	**qäläm**
pencil	**karandash**
postcard	**posht kartı**
scissors	**qaychı**
writing paper	**yazmaq üchün kaghız**

Do you have any foreign publications?	**Sizdä här hansı khariji näshrlär varmı?**

PHOTOGRAPHY

How much is it to process (and print) this film?	**Bu lenti aydınlashdırıb shäkilläri chap etmäk nechäyädir?**

When will it be ready?	**Nä zaman hazır olajaq?**
I'd like film for this camera.	**Män bu fotoaparat üchün lent (plyonka) istäyiräm.**
B&W (film)	**agh-qara plyonka**
camera	**fotoaparat; kamera**
color (film)	**rängli plyonka (lent)**
film	**plyonka; lent**
flash	**ishıq; flash**
lens	**linza**
light meter	**ishıq güjünü ölchän jihaz**

SMOKING

Cigarettes are usually purchased from kiosks. American brands are more pricy but still a bargain by western standards. Best value is to buy by the carton where prices are normally fixed. It is also possible to buy cigarettes in singles. Azerbaijanis will smoke anywhere – it is rare indeed to find a smoke-free area and it is advisable to avoid constricted enclosed places if smoking creates problems for your health or if you simply find it offensive.

A packet of cigarettes, please.	**Bir pachka siqaret verin, zähmät olmasa.**
Are these cigarettes strong/mild?	**Bu siqaret tüntdürmü/ yumshaqdırmı?**
Do you have a light?	**Yumshaq siqaretlärdän varmı?**
Do you have any American cigarettes?	**Amerika siqaretlärindän varmı?**

cigar	**siqara**
cigarette papers	**siqaret kaghızı**
cigarettes	**siqaret(lär)**
a carton of cigarettes	**bir pachka siqaret**
filtered	**filtrli**
filterless	**filtrsiz**
flint	**müshtük**
lighter fluid	**alıshqan yanajaqı**

lighter	**alıshqan**
matches	**kibrit**
menthol	**mentollu**
pipe	**qälyan**
tobacco	**tütün**

ELECTRICAL EQUIPMENT

adapter	**adapter**
battery	**batareya**
cassette	**kaset**
CD	**sidi; kompakt disk**
CD player	**sidi pleyer**
fan	**ventilyator; yelläyän**
hairdryer	**fen; sachqurudan**
heating coil	**elektrik spiral**
iron (for clothing)	**ütü**
kettle	**chaynik; qäfädän**
plug	**razet**
portable TV	**balaja televizor**
radio	**radio**
record	**yazı; musiqi yazızı**
tape (cassette)	**kaset**
tape recorder	**maqnitofon**
television	**televizor**
transformer	**transformator; kechiriji**
video (player)	**videomaqnitofon; videopleyer**
videotape	**videokaset**
voltage regulator	**elektrik gärginliyin nizamlayıjısı**

SIZES

small	**balaja; kichik**
big	**böyük**
heavy	**aghır**
light	**yüngül**
more	**daha chokh**
less	**daha az**
many	**bir chokh**

too much	**häddindän artıgh chokh**
too many	**häddindän artıgh chokh**
enough	**kifayätdir**
that's enough	**bu käfayätdir; bäsdir**
also	**bundan bashqa; hämchinin**
a little bit	**bir az**

| Do you have a carrier bag? | **Sizdä dashımaq üchün chanta (paket) varmı?** |

SHOPS AND MARKETS

When to shop – Shops open around 10.00 am and close around 7.30 pm. New private shops tend not to break for lunch, while older state shops do. Markets are open every day.

How to pay – Everything is best paid for in cash. Credit cards are increasingly acceptable in the cities but travelers' checks are still difficult to cash (although you can always visit the American Express Travel Center in Baku to do this hassle-free). Many shops now have price tags attached to items but in most places you will have to ask.

Food and wine – As well as the main streets of stores in the town centres, every street seems to have its own small produce kiosk or store. There is also a growing number of specialty shops, including supermarkets where you can buy western products – and some truly excellent winesellers.

Markets – For fresh produce go to a **bazar**, 'market.' Prices and availability of goods are seasonal. As a foreigner, you may occasionally find yourself paying a little more here – but not much! The best time is early morning when everything is at its freshest, particularly for meat and fish. In the evenings you'll get a better price (Azeris call this **akhsham bazarı** which loosely translates as 'last bargain'), but less choice. Many local delicacies can be found here, including smoked sturgeon, caviar, smoked and dried meats, and a veritable plethora of spices, nuts and berries. In Baku, visit the colorful flower markets or the **talkuchka** – markets where you can buy all the usual consumer products at a bargain, from cigarettes to CD-players, from clothing to pirate videos.

11. WHAT'S TO SEE

Do you have a guide-book/local map?	**Sizdä turist kitabchası/yerli khäritä varmı?**
Is there a guide who speaks English?	**Orada ingilisjä danishan gid varmı?**
What are the main attractions?	**Äsas diqqätälayiq yerlär hansılardır?**
What is that?	**Bu nädir?**
How old is it?	**Bunun nechä yashı var?**
May I take a photograph?	**Bunun shäklini chäkmäk olarmi?**
What time does it open?	**Bu nä zaman achılır?**
What time does it close?	**Bu nä zaman baghlanır?**
What is this monument/statue?	**Bu abidä/heykäl nädir?**
What does that say?	**Burada nä yazılıb?**
Who is that statue of?	**Bu kimin heykälidir?**
Is there an entrance fee?	**Girish pulladırmı?**
How much?	**Nä qädär?**
Are there any night clubs/discoteques?	**Orada gejä klubları/diskotekalar varmı?**
Where can I hear local folk music?	**Män yerli khalq musiqisini harada eshidä biläräm?**
How much does it cost to get in?	**Ichäri dakhil olmaq nechäyädir?**
What's there to do in the evening?	**Orada akhshamlar nä edirlär?**
Is there a concert?	**Orada konsert varmı?**
When is the wedding?	**Toy nä zamandır?**
What time does it begin?	**O, nä zaman bashlanır?**
Can we swim here?	**Burada chimmäk olarmi?**

ballet	**balet**
blues	**blyuz**
classical music	**klassik musiqi**
dancing	**räqs**
disco	**disko**
disk jockey	**disk zhokey**
elevator	**lift**
escalator	**eskalator**
exhibition	**särgi**
folk dancing	**khalq räqsi**
folk music	**khalq musiqisi**
jazz	**jaz**
lift	**lift**
nightclub	**gejä klubu; diskoteka**
opera	**opera**
party	**shänlik; qonaqlıq**
pub	**piväkhana; pab**
rock concert	**rok musiqisi konserti**
rock 'n' roll	**rok-end-rol**
take-out	**müshahidä etmäk**

BUILDINGS

academy of sciences	**Elmlär Akademiyası**
apartment	**mänzil**
archaeological	**arkheolozhi**
art gallery	**injäsäänät qalereyası**
bakery	**chöräkkhana**
bar	**bar**
apartment block	**yashayısh evi**
building	**bina**
casino	**kazino; qumarkhana**
castle	**qala**
cemetery	**qäbiristanlıq**
church	**kilsä**
cinema	**kinoteatr**
city map	**shähärin khäritäsi**

college	**kollej**
concert hall	**konsert zalı**
concert	**konsert**
embassy	**säfirlik**
hospital	**khästäkhana**
house	**ev**
housing estate/project	**kvartal; mähällä**
library	**kitabkhana**
main square	**bash meydan**
market	**bazar**
monastery	**monastır**
monument	**mä'bäd**
mosque	**mäschid**
museum	**muzey**
old city	**köhnä shähär;**
	In Baku: **İchäri Shähär**
opera house	**opera teatrı**
park	**park**
parliament (building)	**parlament binası;**
	Milli Mäjlis binası
restaurant	**restoran**
ruins	**daghıntılar**
saint's tomb	**seyyid mäzarı pir**
'salon' shop	**salon-maghaza**
school	**mäktäb**
shop	**maghaza; dükan**
shrine	**ibadätgah; müqäddäs yer**
stadium	**stadion**
statue	**heykäl**
synagogue	**sinaqoq**
temple	**kichik kilsä; sovmää**
theater	**teatr**
tomb	**mäzar**
tower	**bürj; güllä**
university	**universitet**
zoo	**zoopark**

OCCASIONS

birth	**anadan olma; doghum**
death	**ölüm**
funeral	**däfnetmä märasimi**
marriage	**toy**

RELIGIOUS HERITAGE

The Azerbaijanis are for the most part nominally Shi'i Muslims. Aside from mosques, you will also discover a few churches or synagogues.

Mosques and madrasas ('religious schools') have always played an important part in the development of the Azerbaijani people and state, and, although the Soviets and demands of modern times have greatly undermined its power and influence, Islam still makes its presence felt through the often stunning religious buildings still standing throughout the country. Of particular significance are the **Göy Mäschid** or 'Blue Mosque,' and the **Täzä Pir** or 'New Mosque,' both in Baku.

Holidays & festivals – There are a wide variety of traditional festivals celebrated in every village and area. Important dates in the national calendar are **Ramazan** (Ramadan), **Kurban Bayram** (Id al-Fitr), **Mähärrämlik** (the Shi'i 'Month of Mourning') and **Novruz Bayramı** — New Year or Spring Festival (March 21st). Because of the influence of European and Russian (Soviet) tradition, New Year (December 31st/January 1st) celebrations have also become one of the major festivities.

12. FINANCE

Currencies – The official currency in Azerbaijan is the **manat**, divided into 100 **qäpiks**. Unofficially in use, but still accepted everywhere outside of government establishments and retail outlets, are U.S. dollars. These may be refused however if notes are creased, torn, old, or simply a low denomination. Be prepared to accept change in **manats**.

Changing money – Aside from the banks, money can also be changed in any bureau de change, where you will find reliable, up-to-date exchange rates prominently displayed on a board. The cashiers will often know a European language or two, and almost all will show the workings of the exchange on a calculator for you and give you a receipt. Many shops and kiosks will also be happy to change money for you.

I want to change some dollars.	**Män bir az dollar däyishmäk istäyiräm.**
I want to change some pounds.	**Män bir az funt sterlinq däyishmäk istäyiräm.**
Where can I change some money?	**Män harada pul däyishä biläräm?**
What is the exchange rate?	**Däyishmä mäzännäsi nädir?**
What is the commission?	**Komissiya faizi nä qädärdir?**
Could you please check that again?	**Zähmät olmasa, bunu bir dä yokhlayın.**
dollar	**dolar**
franc	**frank**
mark	**marka**
ruble	**rubl**
sterling	**funt sterlinq**
bank notes	**kaghız pulu**
calculator	**kalkulyator**

cashier	**kassir**
coins	**dämir pulu**
credit card	**kredit kartı**
commission	**komissiya faizi**
exchange	**däyishmä**
loose change	**khırda pul**
signature	**imza**

COURTESY

Azerbaijanis are a courteous people and this is reflected in the expressions they use towards guests and superiors. Some related expressions you'll commonly hear are:

Welcome!	**Khosh gälmisiniz!**
May you always be our guests!	**Hämishä siz gäläsiz!**
May Allah be good to you!	**Allah razı olsun!**
Respect to our guest!	**Qonagha hörmät!**
Honourable mister . . .	**Möhtäräm Jänab . . .**
Respectable Mr. . . .	**Hörmätli Jänab . . .**
Respectable Mrs. (Ms.) . . .	**Hörmätli Khanım . . .**
Dear . . .	**Äziz . . .**

'His Excellency' is **Zati Aliläri**; while the Sheikh-ul-Islam, or Islamic religious leader of Azerbaijan is addressed as **Sheykh Häzrätläri**.

Useful formulas for toasting at the dinner table using **Bu badäläri qaldıragh . . . saghlıqına!** — 'So let's raise our glasses to the health of . . . !' — are:

to our host	**ev sahibi**
to the organizer of this event	**tädbirin täshkilatchısı**
to the Azerbaijani people	**Azärbayjan khalqının saghlıqına.**

13. COMMUNICATIONS

Telecommunications – All local calls are free, although you need to use tokens in public phones. International calls are dialed direct, or else booked through the international operator – this may incur a wait of several hours. Phones give one long ring to indicate a local call, two shorter rings for an international call. Satellite telephone links are costly but are a reliable and secure method of communication. Pagers and mobile phones are widely used (including GSM). Mobile phones may be rented for a period of time.

Where is the post office?	**Pocht haradadır?**
What time does the post office open?	**Pocht nä zaman achılır?**
What time does the post office close?	**Pocht nä zaman baghlanır?**
Where is the mail box?	**Pocht qutusu haradadır?**
Is there any mail for me?	**Mänim üchün mäktub varmı?**
How long will it take for this to get there?	**Bu oraya hansı müddätä chatajaq?**
How much does it cost to send this to . . . ?	**Bunu . . . göndärmäk üchün nä qädär pul vermäk lazımdır?**
I would like some stamps.	**Mänä bir nechä dänä marka lazımdır.**

I would like to send . . .	**Män . . . göndärmäk istärdim.**
a letter	**mäktub**
a postcard	**pocht kartochkası**
a parcel	**posılka**
a telegram	**teleqram**

air mail	**aviapocht; täyyarä pochtu**
envelope	**zärf**
mailbox	**pocht qutusu**
parcel	**posılka**
registered mail	**sifarishli mäktub**
stamp	**marka**
telegram	**teleqram**

TELE-ETIQUETTE

I would like to make a phone call.	**Män zäng etmäk istärdim.**
I would like to send a fax.	**Män faks göndärmäk istärdim.**
I would like to send a telex.	**Män teleks göndärmäk istärdim.**
Where is the telephone?	**Telefon haradadır?**
May I use your phone?	**Män sizin telefondan istifadä edä bilärämmi?**
Can I telephone from here?	**Män buradan zäng vura bilärämmi?**
Can you help me get this number?	**Siz mänä bu nömräni yıghmagha kömäk edärsinizmi?**
Can you help me get this number?	**Bu nömräni yıghmagha mänä kömäk edärsinizmi?**
Can I dial direct?	**Birbasha yıgha bilärämmi?**
May I speak to Mr. . . . ?	**Män jänab . . . danısha bilärämmi?**
May I speak to Ms./Mrs. . . . ?	**Män khanım . . . danısha bilärämmi?**
Can I leave a message?	**Ona deyiläsi sözüm var, chatdırarsınızmı?**
Who is calling, please?	**Baghıshlayın, kimdir sorushan?**
Who are you calling?	**Sizä kim lazımdır?**
Can I take your name?	**Adınızı ala bilärämmi?**
Which number are you dialling?	**Siz hansı nömräni yıghırsınız?**
He/She is not here at the moment, would you like to leave a message?	**O indi otaghda yokhdur, gäländä ona nä deyim?**
This is not . . .	**Bura . . . deyil.**
You are mistaken.	**Siz säf düshmüsünüz.**
This is the . . . office.	**Bura . . . nümayändäliyidir!**

Hello, I need to speak to . . .	**Allo, salam, mänä . . . lazımdır.**
I am calling this number . . .	**Män . . . nümräni yığhıram.**
The telephone is switched off.	**Telefon söndürülüb.**
I want to ring . . .	**Män . . . zäng etmäk istäyiräm.**
What is the code for . . . ?	**. . . kodu hansıdır?**
What is the international code?	**Beynälkhalq kod hansıdır?**
The number is . . .	**Nömrä budur . . .**
The extension is . . .	**Älavä nömrä budur . . .**
It's busy.	**O mäshquldur.**
I've been cut off.	**Söhbätimi käsdilär.**
The lines have been cut.	**Khättlär käsilib.**
Where is the nearest public phone?	**Än yakhın telefon-avtomat haradadır?**
digital	**räqämli**
e-mail	**elektron pochtu**
fax	**faks**
fax machine	**faks mashını**
handset	**dästäy**
international operator	**beynälkhalq operator**
Internet	**internet**
line	**khätt**
mobile phone	**jib telefonu; mobil telefon**
modem	**modem**
operator	**telefonchu**
satellite phone	**peyk telefonu**
telephone center	**telefon stansiyası**
telex	**teleks**
to transfer/put through	**jalashdırmaq**

14. THE OFFICE

chair	**kürsü; oturajaq**
computer	**kompüter; bilgisayar**
desk	**masa**
drawer	**räf**
fax	**faks**
file	*paper* **qovluq**
	computer **fayl**
meeting	**görüsh**
paper	**kaghız**
pen	**qäläm**
pencil	**karandash**
photocopier	**kopiya mashını; sürät chıkharma mashını; kseroks**
photocopy	**fotosürät**
printer	**printer; kompyuter chap mashını**
report	**hesabat**
ruler	**khätkesh**
telephone	**telefon**
telex	**teleks**
typewriter	**chap mashını**

Electric current – Because of different means of generating power, the current still varies across the country. The supply, in any case, may not be constantly at full voltage and lengthy power failures may be common, particularly in winter. Although many buildings will now have their own back-up generators in case of power failure, be sure to keep a torch or supply of candles.

15. THE CONFERENCE

article	**mäqalä**
a break for refreshments	**qısa chay fasiläsi**
conference room	**konfrans otaghı**
copy	**sürät**
discussion	**müzakirä**
forum	**forum; yıghınjaq; mäjlis**
guest speaker	**dä'vät olunmush mä'ruzächi**
a paper	**kaghız**
podium	**podium**
projector	**proyektor**
session	**sessiya**
a session chaired by . . .	**sessiyanın sädri . . . idi**
speaker	**sädr; spiker**
subject	**mövzu**

MORE TELE-ETIQUETTE

Common ways of answering the phone:

Yes?	**Bäli?**
Hello?	**Allo?**
Please!	**Buyurunuz!**

YES & NO

YES – There are three words for yes: **bäli!** – a neutral, polite form; **hä!** – which is more informal; and, although not strictly the same as 'yes' in English, **var** means 'yes, there is/are.'

NO – Azerbaijanis have more than one word for 'no', again used according to context: **kheyr!** 'no!' and **yokh!** 'no there isn't/aren't'.

16. THE FARM

agriculture	**känd täsärrufatı**
barley	**arpa**
barn	**päyä**
cattle	**iri buynuzlu heyvanlar**
to clear land	**torpagh sahäsini tämizlämäk**
combine harvester	**takhıl kombaynı**
corn	**qarghudalı**
crops	**äkin sahäläri**
earth	**torpagh**
fallowland	**herik sahä**
farm	**ferma**
farmer	**fermer; känd täsärrufatchısı**
farming	**ferma täsärrufatchılıghı**
(animal) feed	**yem**
fertilizer	**peyin**
field	**sahä**
fruit	**meyvä**
garden	**bagh**
to grow crops	**mähsul yetishtirmäk**
harvest	**mähsul**
hay	**ot**
haystack	**taya**
marsh	**qamıshlıq**
mill	**däyirman**
orchard	**bagh**
planting	**äkin; säpin**
plow	**kotan**
to plow	**shumlamaq**
reaping	**bichin**
season	**mövsum; fäsil**
seed	**tokhum; takhil**
sowing	**tokhum etmäk**
tractor	**traktor**
wheat	**chovdar**
well (of water)	**(artezian) quyu**

17. ANIMALS

MAMMALS

bear	ayı
bull	gamish
cat	pishik
cow	inäk
deer	maral
dog	it
donkey	eshshäk
flock	sürü; nakhır
goat	kechi
herd	sürü
horse	at
lamb	quzu
mare	madyan
mouse	sichan
mule	qatır
pig	donuz
pony	poni
rabbit	dovshan
ram	qoch
rat	sichovul
sheep	qoyun
sheepdog	chobaniti; alabash
stallion	ayghır
wolf	qurt

BIRDS

bird	qush
chicken/hen	toyuq
crow	qargha
duck	ördäk
eagle	qartal
goose	qaz
owl	bayqush

partridge	**käklik**
rooster	**khoruz**
turkey	**hindushka; hind toyughu**

INSECTS & AMPHIBIANS

ant	**qarıshka**
bee	**ari**
butterfly	**käpänäk**
caterpillar	**tırtıl**
cockroach	**tarakan; mätbäkhböjäyi**
fish	**balıgh**
flea	**bit**
fleas	**bitlär**
fly	**qara milchäk**
frog	**qurbagha**
insect	**häsharat**
lizard	**kärtänkälä**
louse	**bit**
mosquito	**aghjaqanad**
snail	**ilbiz**
snake	**ilan**
spider	**hörümchäk**
termite	**qarıshka**
tick	**känä**
wasp	**eshshäkarısı**
worm	**qurd**

18. COUNTRYSIDE

avalanche	**qar uchghunu; chıgh**
canal	**kanal**
cave	**maghara; kaha; zagha**
dam	**damba**
earthquake	**zälzälä**
fire	**yanghın**
flood	**dashqın**
foothills	**dagh ätäyi**
footpath	**jıghır**
forest	**meshä**
hill	**täpä**
lake	**göl**
landslide	**chökmä; torpaq sürüshmäsi**
mountain	**dagh**
mountain pass	**dagh yolu; ashırım**
peak	**zirvä; pik**
plain	**düzänlik**
plant	**bitki**
range	**mäsafä**
ravine	**yarghan**
river bank	**chay sahili**
river	**chay**
rock	**qaya**
slope	**daghın döshü; yamaj**
stream	**akhin**
summit	**zirvä**
swamp	**bataghlıq**
tree	**aghaj**
valley	**vadi**
waterfall	**shälalä**
a wood	**aghajlıq**

19. THE WEATHER

Azerbaijan enjoys nine wholly distinct climate zones, ranging from the subtropical to alpine — which is not surprising if you consider its varied terrain. In the coastal plains in the eastern part of the country towards the Caspian Sea the winters are mild and the summers hot and sticky. In the forested hill country to the west, all four seasons tend to be clearly defined, with brilliant springs, balmy summers, golden autumns and crisp winters. The mountain slopes to the north have cool summers and harsh winters which result in some areas being snowed in for much of the year.

What's the weather like?	**Havalar nejädir?**
The weather is . . . today.	**Bu gün hava . . . -dir.**

cold	**soyuq**
cool/fresh	**särin**
cloudy	**buludlu**
foggy	**dumanlı**
freezing	**shakhtali; bärk soyuq**
hot	**isti**
misty	**dumanlı**
very hot	**chokh isti**
windy	**küläkli**

It's going to rain.	**Yaghısh olajaqdır.**
It is raining.	**Yaghısh yaghır.**
It's going to snow.	**Qar olajaq.**
It is snowing.	**Qar yaghır.**
It is sunny.	**Günäshlidir.**

air	**hava; säma**
cloud	**bulud**
fog	**duman**
frost	**shakhta**

full moon	**mehtab**
heatwave	**istilik dalghası**
ice	**buz**
midsummer	**yayın ortası**
midwinter	**qıshiın ortası**
mild winter	**yumshaq qısh**
moon	**ay**
new moon	**tәzә ay**
rain	**yaghısh**
severe winter	**aghır qısh**
sleet	**boran**
snow	**qar**
solstice	**sırsıra; buz baghlama**
star	**ulduz**
sun	**günäsh**
sunny	**günäshli**
thaw	**yumshaq hava**
weather	**hava**
spring	**yaz**
summer	**yay**
autumn	**payız**
winter	**qısh**

20. CAMPING

Where can we camp?	**Düshärgäni harada qura bilärik?**
Can we camp here?	**Burada düshärgä qurmaq olarmı?**
Is it safe to camp here?	**Burada düshärgä qurmaq tählükäsizdirmi?**
Is there drinking water?	**Orada ichmäli su varmı?**
May we light a fire?	**Biz od qalaya bilärikmi?**

axe	**balta**
backpack	**baghlama**
bucket	**vedrä**
campsite	**düshärgä yeri**
can opener	**konserva achan**
compass	**kompas**
firewood	**odun; chör-chöp**
flashlight	**fänär; prozhektor**
gas canister	**qaz balonu**
hammer	**chäkij**
ice axe	**buz baltası**
lamp	**lampa**
mattress	**döshäk** (*pronounced* 'döshäy')
penknife	**jib bıjaghı**
rope	**kändir**
sleeping bag	**yataqli torba**
stove	**ojaq**
tent	**chadır**
tent pegs	**payachıq**
water bottle	**su shüshäsi**

21. IN CASE OF EMERGENCY

Complaining — If you really feel you have been cheated or misled, raise the matter first with your host or the proprietor of the establishment in question, preferably with a smile. Azerbaijanis are proud but courteous, with a deeply felt tradition of hospitality, and consider it their duty to help any guest. Angry glares and shouting will get you nowhere.

Crime — Azerbaijanis are law-abiding people, but petty theft does occur. Without undue paranoia, take usual precautions: watch your wallet or purse, securely lock your equipment and baggage before handing it over to railway or airline porters, and don't leave valuables on display in your hotel room. If you are robbed, contact the police. Of course, in the more remote areas sensible precautions should be taken and always ensure that you go with a guide. In general, follow the same rules as you would in your own country and you will run little risk of encountering crime.

What to do if you lose something — Save time and energy by appealing only to senior members of staff or officials. If you have lost items in the street or left anything in public transport, the police may be able to help.

Disabled facilities — The terrain and conditions throughout most of Azerbaijan do not make it easy for any visitor to get around in a wheelchair even at the best of times. Access to most buildings in the cities is difficult, particularly since the majority of lifts function irregularly. Facilities are rarely available in hotels, airports or other public areas.

Toilets — You will find public utilities located in any important or official building. You may use those in hotels or restaurants. You may sometimes encounter failed plumbing and absence of toilet paper. Similar to Turkey and countries in the Middle East, people in Azerbaijan tend to use water from a conveniently positioned faucet or jug instead of toilet paper.

wheelchair	**täkärli oturajag**
disabled	**älil; shikäst**
Do you have seats for the disabled?	**Sizdä älillär üchün yerlär varmı?**
Do you have access for the disabled?	**Sizdä älillär üchün girish varmı?**

Do you have facilities for the disabled?	**Sizdä älillär üchün shärait yaradılıbmı?**
Help!	**Kömäk edin!**
Could you help me, please?	**Khahish ediräm, mänä kömäk edäsiniz.**
Do you have a telephone?	**Sizdä telefon varmı?**
Can I use your telephone?	**Sizin telefonuzdan istifadä edä bilärämmi?**
Where is the nearest telephone?	**Än yakhında olan telefon haradadır?**
Does the phone work?	**Telefon ishläyirmi?**
Get help quickly!	**Tez ol, kömäk chaghır!**
Call the police.	**Polisä zäng vur.**
I'll call the police!	**Män polisä zäng vurajam!**
Is there a doctor near here?	**Yakhında häkim varmı?**
Call a doctor.	**Häkim chaghır.**
Call an ambulance.	**Tä'jili yardım chaghır.**
I'll get medical help!	**Män tibbi yardım täshkil edäjäyäm/edäjäm.**
Where is the doctor?	**Häkim haradadır?**
Where is the hospital?	**Khästäkhana haradadır?**
Where is the pharmacy?	**Äjzakhana haradadır?**
Where is the dentist?	**Dish häkimi haradadır?**
Where is the police station?	**Polis shö'bäsi haradadır?**
Take me to a doctor.	**Mäni häkimin yanına apar.**
There's been an accident!	**Orada hadisä bash verib!**
Is anyone hurt?	**Khäsärät alan varmı?**
This person is hurt.	**Bu adam yaralanıb.**
There are people injured.	**Yaralananlar var.**
Don't move!	**Tärpänmä!**
Go away!	**Chäkıl!; Chıkh get!**
I am lost.	**Män yolumu itirmishäm.**
I am ill.	**Män khästäyäm.**
I've been raped.	**Mäni zorlayıblar.**

I've been robbed.	**Mäni soyublar.**
Thief!	**Oghru!**
My . . . has been stolen.	**Mänim . . . oghurlanıb.**
I have lost . . .	**Män . . . itirmishäm.**
my bags	**chantalarımı**
my camera equipment	**fotokamera avadanlıghımı**
my handbag	**äl chantamı**
my laptop computer	**laptop kompüterimi**
my money	**pulumu**
my passport	**pasportumu**
my sound equipment	**säs yazma avadanlıghımı**
my travelers' checks	**bank cheklärimi**
my wallet	**pul kisämi**
My possessions are insured.	**Mänim shäkhsi äshyalarım sıghortalanıb.**
I have a problem.	**Mänim problemim var.**
I didn't do it.	**Män bunu etmämishäm.**
I'm sorry.	**Män täässüf ediräm.**
I apologize.	**Män sizdän üzr istäyiräm.**
I didn't realize anything was wrong.	**Män näyinsä düz olmadıghını basha düshmädim.**
I want to contact my embassy.	**Män säfirliyimizlä älaqä sakhlamaq istäyiräm.**
I want to contact my consulate.	**Män konsulluqumuzla älaqä sakhlamaq istäyiräm.**
I speak English.	**Män Ingilisjä danıshıram.**
I need an interpreter.	**Mänä tärjümächi lazımdır.**
Where are the toilets?	**Tualetlär haradadır?**

22. HEALTHCARE

Health/medical information — Make sure any insurance policy you take out covers Azerbaijan, although this will only help in flying you out in case of a serious accident or illness. No vaccinations are required for Azerbaijan, although your doctor may suggest you take the boosters usually recommended when making any trip outside of North America and Western Europe.

Pharmacies are easy to find but can be understocked at times. If planning to travel off the beaten track, it is probably best to bring a sufficient supply of any specific medication you require. But most of the familiar range of medicines can be found in the capital Baku, in chain supermarkets like Ramstore, and numerous smaller stores. Don't forget to check the 'best before' date.

What's the trouble?	**Nä bash verib?**
I am sick.	**Män khästälänmishäm.**
My companion is sick.	**Mänim yoldashım khästälänib.**
May I see a female doctor?	**Män khanım häkimi görä bilärämmi?**
I have medical insurance.	**Mänim tibbi sıghortam vardir.**
Please undress.	**Khahish ediräm, soyunun.**
How long have you had this problem?	**Bu väziyyät nä qädär vakht davam edir?**
How long have you been feeling sick?	**Siz özünüzü nä qädär vakht khästä hiss edirsiniz?**
Where does it hurt?	**Haranız aghrıyır?**
It hurts here.	**Buram aghrıyır.**
I have been vomiting.	**Män qusmusham.**
I feel dizzy.	**Bashım gijälänir.**
I can't eat.	**Män yemäk yeyä bilmiräm.**
I can't sleep.	**Män yata bilmiräm.**
I feel worse.	**Män özümü daha pis hiss ediräm.**
I feel better.	**Män özümü daha yakhshı hiss ediräm.**

I have . . .	**Mändä . . . vardır.**
Do you have . . . ?	*familiar* **Sändä . . . varmı?**
	polite **Sizdä . . . varmı?**
diabetes	**diabet; shäkär khästäliyi**
epilepsy	**tutma; epilepsiya**
asthma	**astma**
I'm pregnant.	**Män boyluyam.;**
	Män hamiläyäm.
I have. . .	**Mändä . . . var.**
a cold	**soyuqdäymä**
a cough	**ösküräk**
a headache	**bash aghrısı**
a pain	**aghrı**
a sore throat	**boghaz aghrısı**
a temperature	**qızdırma**
an allergy	**allergiya**
an infection	**yolukhma; infeksiya**
an itch	**qashınma**
backache	**bel aghrısı**
constipation	**qäbälik**
diarrhea	**ishal**
fever	**qızdırma; isitmä**
hepatitis	**sarılıq**
indigestion	**mä'dä pozghunluqu**
influenza	**qrip**
a heart condition	**üräk khästäliyi**
pins and needles	**iynälär**
stomachache	**qarın aghrısı**
a fracture	**sınıq**
toothache	**dish aghrısı**
You have . . .	**Sizdä . . . var.**
a cold	**soyuqdäymä**
a cough	**ösküräk**

a headache	**bash aghrısı**
a pain	**aghrı**
a sore throat	**boghaz aghrısı**
a temperature	**qızdırma**
an allergy	**allergiya**
an infection	**infeksiya; yolukhma**
an itch	**qashınma**
backache	**bel aghrısı**
constipation	**qäbälik**
diarrhea	**ishal**
fever	**isitmä**
hepatitis	**sarılıq khästäliyi**
indigestion	**mä'dä pozghunluqu**
influenza	**qrip**
a heart condition	**uräk khästäliyi**
pins and needles	**iynälär**
stomachache	**qarın aghrısı**
a fracture	**sınma**
toothache	**dish aghrısı**

I take this medication.	**Män bu därmanı qäbul ediräm.**
I need medication for...	**Mänä ... üchün därman lazımdır.**
What type of medication is this?	**Bu hansı növlü därmandır?**
How many times a day must I take it?	**Män bunu gündä nechä däfä qäbul etmäliyäm?**
When should I stop?	**Män näzaman qäbul etmäni sakhlamalıyam?**
I'm on antibiotics.	**Män antibiotiklär qäbul ediräm.**
I'm allergic to...	**Mänim ... qarshı allergiyam var.**
antibiotics	**antibiotiklär**
penicillin	**penisilin**
I have been vaccinated.	**Män peyvänd olunmusham.**

I have my own syringe.	**Mänim öz iynäm var.**
Is it possible for me to travel?	**Män säfär edä bilärämmi?**

HEALTH WORDS

aspirin	**aspirin**
antibiotic	**antibiotik**
AIDS	**Eyds khästäliyi; Spid khästäliyi**
alcoholic	**ichki düshkünü; äyyash**
alcoholism	**äyyashlıq**
amputation	**amputasiya**
anemia	**qan chatıshmazlıqı**
anesthetic	**keyläshdiriji**
anesthetist	**anesteziyachi**
antibiotic	**antibiotik**
antiseptic	**antiseptik**
blood	**qan**
blood group	**qan qrupu**
blood pressure:	**qan täzyiqi**
low blood pressure	**ashaqı qan täzyiqi**
high blood pressure	**yüksäk qan täzyiqi**
blood transfusion	**qan köchürülmäsi**
bone	**sümük**
cancer	**khärchäng**
cholera	**väba**
clinic	**klinika; khästäkhana**
dentist	**dish häkimi**
drug	**därman;** *narcotic* **uyushduruju maddä**
epidemic	**epidemiya**
fever	**isitmä**
flu	**qrip; soyuqdäymä**
frostbite	**donma**
germs	**mıkrob**
heart attack	**üräk tutması**

hygiene	**gigiyena; tämizlik**
infection	**infeksiya**
limbs	**äl-ayaq**
needle	**iynä**
nurse	**tibb bajısı**
operating room	**järrahiyyä ämäliyyatı otaghı**
(surgical) operation	**järrahiyyä ämäliyyatı**
oxygen	**oksigen**
painkiller	**aghrıkäsän därman**
physiotherapy	**fizioterapiya**
rabies	**quduzluq**
shrapnel	**qälpä**
sleeping pill	**yukhu därmanı**
snake bite	**ilan dishlämäsi**
stethoscope	**stetoskop**
surgeon	**järrah**
(act of) surgery	**järrahiyyä ämäliyyatı**
syringe	**iynä**
thermometer	**termometr; istilikölchän**
torture	**ishkänjä**
tranquilizer	**sakitläshdiriji; aghrıkäsän**

I have broken my glasses.	**Män eynäyimi sındırmısham.**
Can you repair them?	**Siz onu däzäldä bilärsinizmi?**
I need new lenses.	**Mänä yeni shüshälär lazımdır.**
When will they be ready?	**Onlar nä zaman hazır olajaq?**
How much do I owe you?	**Män sizä nä qädär borjluyam?**

contact lenses	**kontakt linzaları**
contact lens solution	**kontakt linzaları üchün tämizläyiji**

23. RELIEF AID

Can you help me?	**Siz mänä kömäk edä bilärsinizmi?**
Do you speak English?	**Siz ingilisjä danıshırsınızmı?**
Who is in charge?	**Burada rähbär kimdir?**
Fetch the main person in charge.	**Buranın rähbärini tapın.**
What's the name of this town?	**Bu shähärin adı nädir?**
How many people live there?	**Burada nä qädär adam yashayır?** *or* **Shähärin nä qädär ähalisi var?**
What's the name of that river?	**O chayın adı nädir?**
How deep is it?	**Onun därinliyi nä qädärdir?**
Is the bridge still standing?	**O körpu hälä dururmu?**
What is the name of that mountain?	**Bu daghın adı nädir?**
How high is it?	**Onun yüksäkliyi nä qädärdir?**
Where is the border?	**Särhäd hansı täräfdädir?**
Is it safe?	**Ora tählükäsizdirmi?**
Show me.	**Onu mänä göstär.**

CHECKPOINTS

checkpoint	**yokhlama mäntäqäsi**
roadblock	**yol postu**
Stop!	**Dayan!**
Do not move!	**Tärpänmä!**
Go!	**Get!**
Who are you?	**Sän kimsän?**
Don't shoot!	**Atäsh achmayın!**

Help!	**Kömäk edin!**
no entry	**girish qadaghandır**
emergency exit	**avariya chıkhıshı**
straight on	**düz**
turn left	**sola dön**
turn right	**sagha dön**
this way	**bu täräfä; bu yol ilä**
that way	**o täräfä; o yol ilä**

Keep quiet!	**Sakit ol!**
You are right.	**Siz haqlısınız!**
You are wrong.	**Siz yanlıshsınız!**
I am ready.	**Män hazıram.**
I am in a hurry.	**Män täläsiräm.**
Well, thank you!	**Oldu, täshäkkür ediräm!**
What's that?	**Bu nädir?**
Come in!	**Gälin ichäri!**
That's all!	**Bu qädär!**

FOOD DISTRIBUTION

feeding station	**yemäk stansiyasi**
How many people in your family?	**Ailänizdä nechä adam var?**
How many children?	**Nechä ushaqınız var?**
You must come back this afternoon.	**Siz . . . qayıtmalısınız.** **bu gün**
tonight	**bu akhsham**
tomorrow	**sabah**
the day after	**bur gün sonra**
next week	**gälän häftä**

There is water for you.	**Bu su sizin üchündir.**
There is grain for you.	**Bu takhil sizin üchündir.**
There is food for you.	**Bu ärzaq sizin üchündir.**
There is fuel for you.	**Bu yanajaq sizin üchündir.**

ROAD REPAIR

Is the road passable?	**O yoldan kechmäk mümkündürmü?**
Is the road blocked?	**O yol baghlıdırmı?**
We are repairing the road.	**Biz bu yolu düzäldirik.**
We are repairing the bridge.	**Biz körpünü düzäldirik.**
We need . . .	**Bizä . . . lazımdır.**
wood	**takhta**
rock	**dash**
gravel	**jınqıl**
sand	**qum**
fuel	**yanajaq**

MINES

mine *noun*	**mina**
mines	**minalar**
mine *adjective*	**mänimki**
minefield	**minalanmısh sahä**
to lay mines	**mina yatızdırmaq**
to hit a mine	**minaya düshmäk**
to clear a mine	**minanı zärärsizläshdirmäk**
mine detector	**mina tapan**
mine disposal	**mina tämizläyiji**

Are there any mines near here?	**Burada minalar varmı?**
What type are they?	**Onlar hansı növlüdür?**
anti-vehicle	**mashinlara qarshı**
anti-personnel	**piyadalara qarshı**
plastic	**plastmas**
floating	**üzän**
magnetic	**maqnitli**

What size are they?	**Onlar nä boydadır?**
What color are they?	**Onlar nä rängdädir?**

Are they marked?	**Onlar qeydä alınıbmı?**
How?	**Nejä?**
How many mines are there?	**Orada nechä dänä mina var?**
When were they laid?	**Onlar nä zaman yatızdırılıb?**
Can you take me to the minefields?	**Siz mäni minalanmısh sahäyä apara bilärsinizmi?**
Are there any booby traps near there?	**Buralarda tälä minaları varmı?**
Are they made from grenades, high explosives or something else?	**Onlar toplardan, yuksäk däräjäli partlayıjıdan yokhsa digär maddädän düzäldilib?**
Are they in a building?	**Onlar binanın ichärisindädirlärmi?**
on tracks?	**izlärdädirlärmi?**
on roads?	**yollardadırlärmi?**
on bridges?	**körpülärdädirlärmi?**
or elsewhere?	**yakhud bashqa yerlärdä?**
Can you show me?	**Mänä göstärä bilärsänmi?**

OTHER WORDS

airforce	**härbi hava donanması**
ambulance	**täjili yardım mashını**
armored car	**zirehli mashın**
army	**ordu**
artillery	**artileriya**
barbed wire	**tikanlı mäftil**
bomb	**bomba**
bomber	**bombardman täyyarä**
bullet	**güllä**
cannon	**top**
disaster	**fajiä**
earthquake	**zälzälä**
fighter	**döyüshchü**
gun	**tüfäng**

machine gun	**güllä sachan; pulemyot**
missile	**raket**
missiles	**raketlär**
natural disaster	**täbii fälekät**
navy	**däniz donanması**
nuclear power	**nüvä qüvväsi**
nuclear power station	**nuvä elektrik stansiyası**
officer	**zabit**
parachute	**parashut**
peace	**sülh**
people	**insanlar; adamlar;** *familiar* **jamaat**
pistol	**tapanja**
refugee camp	**qachqinlar düshärgäsi**
refugee	**qachqin**
refugees	**qachqınlar**
relief aid	**yardım**
sack	**kisä**
shell	**märmi**
submachine gun	**avtomat**
tank	**tank**
troops	**qoshunlar**
unexploded bomb	**partlamamısh bomba**
United Nations	**Birläshmish Millätlär Täshkilatı**
war	**müharibä**
weapon	**silah**

24. TOOLS

binoculars	**durbin**
brick	**kärpich**
brush	**fircha; shotka**
cable	**mäftil; kabel**
cooker	**mätbäkh sobası**
drill	**burghu**
eyeglasses	**eynäk**
gas bottle	**qaz balonu**
hammer	**chäkij**
handle	**dästäk**
hose	**shlanq**
insecticide	**insektisid; qurd därmani**
ladder	**pilläkän**
machine	**mashın**
microscope	**mikroskop**
nail	**qadagh**
padlock	**anbar kiliti**
paint	**boya**
pickaxe	**külüng**
plank	**shalban**
plastic	**plastmas**
rope	**kämär**
rubber	**rezin**
rust	**pas**
saw	**mishar**
scissors	**qaychı**
screw	**vint**
screwdriver	**vintburan**
spade	**yaba**
spanner	**achar**
string	**tilov ipi; tel**
sunglasses	**qunä qarshı eynäk**
telescope	**teleskop**
varnish	**lak**
wire	**tel; mäftil**

25. THE CAR

Driving — Unless you already know the country well, it is inadvisable to bring your own vehicle to Azerbaijan. If you do, you will need an international driving license, car registration papers and insurance. You will be able to find spare parts for any vehicle: major international car manufacturers have their dealers in Baku which provide all necessary services for your car. Driving conditions used to be good, although the recent conflicts have taken their predictable toll on the road system. Normally roads are well signposted. But side-roads may give no warning of roadworks and sometimes manholes are not closed properly. Street lighting is sporadic, and traffic lights, if they exist, rarely work and are not always observed. So ensure that you take some caution at red lights and check that the way is clear. Certain areas have parking restrictions, although it is not always obvious where they are or what the restrictions are. Rather than book you, the police will simply remove the license plates of an illegally parked car. The unfortunate driver then has to discover which police unit or station is holding them, and negotiate a suitable fee for their return. But in general you may park your car where you wish, provided that you do not block traffic.

Where can I rent a car?	**Män mashını ijaräyä harada götürä biläräm?**
Where can I rent a car with a driver?	**Män sürüjü ilä mashın harada sifarish edä biläräm.**
How much is it per day?	**Bunu gündälik haqqı nä qädärdir?**
How much is it per week?	**Bunun häftälik haqqı nä qädärdir?**
Can I park here?	**Män burada sakhlaya bilärämmi?**
Are we on the right road for. . .?	**Biz . . . istiqamätindä aparan düz yoldayıqmı?**
Where is the nearest filling station?	**Än yakhın yanajaq mäntäqäsi yaradadır?**

Fill the tank please.	**Khahish ediräm, bakı doldurasınız.**
normal/diesel	**normal/dizel**
Check the oil/tires/ battery, please.	**Khahish ediräm, yanajaghı/ täkärläri/akumulyatoru yokhlayasınız.**

I've broken down.	**Mühärrik kharab olub.**
I have a puncture.	**Täkär deshilib.**
I have run out of gas.	**Yanajaq qurtarıb.**
Our car is stuck.	**Mashınımız ilishib qalıb.**
There's something wrong with this car.	**Bu mashında nä isä düz ishlämir.**
We need a mechanic.	**Bizä mekhanik lazımdır.**
Can you tow us?	**Bizi qoshub apara bilärsinizmi?**
Where is the nearest garage?	**Burada än yakhın mashın tä'miri haradadır?**
Can you jumpstart the car?	**Itäläyib mashını ishä sala bilärsänmi?**
There's been an accident.	**Orada yol-näqliyyat hadisäsi bash verib.**
My car has been stolen.	**Mänim mashınımı qachırdıblar.**
Call the police.	**Polisä zäng vurun.**

CAR WORDS

driving license	**sürüjü väsiqäsi**
insurance policy	**sıghorta sänädi, polis**
car papers	**mashının sänädläri**
car registration	**qeydiyyat nömräsi**
accelerator	**qaz pedalı**
air	**hava**
anti-freeze	**antifriz**
battery	**akumulyator**
bonnet	**kapot**
boot	**baqazh yeri; yük yeri**

brake	**tormoz**
bumper/fender	**bamper**
car park	**avtomobil dayanajaqı**
clutch	**qoshqu**
driver	**sürüjü**
engine	**mühärrik**
exhaust	**ishlänmish qazın chıkhması üchün boru**
fan belt	**yelläyänin kämäri**
gas (petrol)	**benzin**
gear	**ötürüjü; naqil**
indicator light	**indikator ishıqı**
inner-tube	**shin**
jack	**domkrat**
mechanic	**mekhanik**
neutral drive	**neytral**
oil	**mühärrik yaghı**
oilcan	**yagh bankası**
passenger	**särnishin**
petrol (gas)	**benzin**
radiator	**radiator**
reverse	**dal ötürüjüsü**
seat	**oturajaq**
spare tire	**ehtiyaj täkäri**
speed	**sürät**
steering wheel	**sükan**
tank	**bak**
tire	**täkär**
tow rope	**baghlama**
windshield	**qabaq shushä**

26. COLORS

black	**qara**
blue	**qöy**
brown	**qähväyi**
green	**yashil**
orange	**narinji**
pink	**chährayl**
purple	**bänövshäyi**
red	**qırmızı**
white	**agh**
yellow	**sarı**

27. SPORTS

Displays of physical strength are greatly prized in Azerbaijani society. Wrestling and horse-racing are particularly favorite sports. More recent sports adopted include judo and other martial arts, rugby, basketball and, of course, soccer.

athletics	**atletika**
ball	**top**
basketball	**basketbol**
chess	**shakhmat**
goal	**qol**
horse racing	**chıdır**
horse-riding	**at yarıshı**
match	**oyun**
soccer match	**futbol matchı**
pitch	**meydan**
referee	**hakim**
rugby	**reqbi**
skating	**konkı yarıshı**
skiing	**ayaq khizäyi idmanı**
soccer	**futbol**
stadium	**stadion**
swimming	**üzmä**
team	**komanda**
wrestling	**güläsh**

Who won?	**Kim uddu?**
What's the score?	**Hesab nechä oldu?**
Who scored?	**Kim qol vurdu?**

28. THE BODY

ankle	**topuq**
arm	**äl**
back	**bel**
beard	**saqqal**
blood	**qan**
body	**bädän**
bone	**sümük**
bottom	**arkha; dal**
breast/chest	**sinä**
chin	**chänä**
ear	**qulaq**
elbow	**dirsäk**
eye	**göz**
face	**üz**
finger	**barmaq**
foot	**ayaq**
genitals	**jinsi orqanlar**
hair	**sach**
hand	**äl**
head	**bash**
heart	**üräk**
jaw	**chänä**
kidney	**böyräk**
knee	**diz**
leg	**bud**
lip	**dodaq**
liver	**qarajiyär**
lung	**agh jiyär**
mustache	**bıgh**
mouth	**aghız**
neck	**boyun**
nose	**burun**
shoulder	**chiyin**
stomach	**qarın; gödän**

teeth	**dishlär**
throat	**boghaz**
thumb	**böyük barmaq**
toe	**daban**
tongue	**dil**
tooth	**dish**
vein	**vena**
womb	**ushaqlıq**
wrist	**äl**

29. POLITICS

aid worker	**humanitar yardım ishchisi**
ambassador	**säfir**
arrest	**häbs**
assassination	**sui-qäsd**
assembly	**yıghınjaq; mäjlis**
autonomy	**özünü-idarä**
cabinet	**kabinet**
a charity	**kheyriyyächilik**
citizen	**vätändash**
civil rights	**vätändash hüquqları**
civil war	**vätändash müharibäsi**
communism	**komunizm**
communist	**komunist**
concentration camp	**konslaqer; häbs düshärgäsi**
constitution	**konstitusiya; äsas qanun**
convoy	**konvoy; müshaiyät**
corruption	**rüshvätkhorluq**
coup d'état	**dövlät chevrilishi**
crime	**jinayät**
criminal	**jinayätkar**
crisis	**böhran**
dictator	**diktator**
debt	**borj**
democracy	**demokratiya**
dictatorship	**diktatorluq**
diplomatic ties	**diplomatik älaqälär**
election	**sechkilär**
embassy	**säfirlik**
ethnic cleansing	**milli (etnik) tämizlämä**
exile	**sürgün**
free	**azad**
freedom	**azadlıq**
government	**hökumät**
guerrilla	**partizan**

hostage	**äsir**
humanitarian aid	**humanitar yardım**
human rights	**insan hüquqları**
imam	**imam**
independence	**müstägillik**
independent	**müstägil**
independent state	**müstägil dövlät**
judge	**hakim**
killer	**qatil**
law court	**mähkämä**
law	**hüquq**
lawyer	**hüquqshunas; advokat**
leader	**rähbär**
left-wing	**solchu**
liberation	**azad etmä**
majority	**chokhluq**
mercenary	**muzdur**
minister	**nazir**
ministry	**nazirlik**
minority	**azlıq**
murder	**qätl**
opposition	**mükhalifät**
parliament	**parlament;**
	Milli Mäjlis *(in Azerbaijan)*
(political) party	**(siyasi) partiya**
politics	**siyasät**
peace	**sülh**
peace-keeping troops	**sülhü-qoruyuju qüvvälär**
politician	**siyasätchi**
premier	**bash nazir; premyer**
president	**prezident**
presidential guard	**prezident qvardiyası**
prime minister	**bash nazir**
prison	**häbskhana**
prisoner-of-war	**äsir**
POW camp	**äsirlär düshärgäsi**

protest	**protest**
rape	**zorlama**
reactionary	**irtijachı**
Red Crescent	**Qırmızı Aypara**
Red Cross	**Qırmızı Khach**
refugee	**qachqın**
revolution	**inqilab**
right-wing	**saghchı**
robbery	**qarätchilik**
seat (in assembly)	**yer**
secret police	**mäkhfi polis**
socialism	**sosializm**
socialist	**sosialist**
spy	**jasus**
struggle	**mübarizä**
theft	**oghurluq**
trade union	**hämkarlar ittifaqı**
treasury	**khäzinä**
United Nations	**Birläshmish Millätlär Täshkilatı**
veto	**veto; qadaghan**
vote	**säs**
vote-rigging	**säs vermänin sakhtalashdırılması**
voting	**säs vermä**

REFUGEES

The word **qachqın** (*plural* **qachqınlar**) is used as the general word for refugee. Displaced Persons are **mäjbur köchkünlär**.

30. OIL & GAS

barrel	**bochka; chälläk**
crude (oil)	**kham neft**
deepwater platform	**därin sular üchün platforma**
derrick	**vıshka; buruq**
diver	**dalghıj**
drill *noun*	**qazıma mashını**
drill a well	**quyu qazımaq**
drilling	**qazıma**
exploration	**akhtarısh**
fuel	**yanajaq**
gas	**qaz**
gas field	**qaz yataghı**
gas production	**qaz istehsalı**
gas well	**qaz quyusu**
geologist	**geoloq**
laboratory	**laboratoriya**
natural resources	**täbii ehtiyatlar**
off-shore	**dänizdä**
oil	**neft**
oil pipeline	**neft kämäri**
oil production	**neft istehsalı**
oil tanker	**neft tankeri**
oil well	**neft quyusu**
oil worker	**neftchi**
oilfield	**neft yataghı; neft mä'däni**
petroleum	**neft**
platform	**platforma**
pump	**nasos; soruyuju**
pumping station	**nasos mäntäqäsi**
refine	**e'mal etmäk**
refinery	**e'malatkhana; neftayırma muässisäsi**
reserves	**ehtiyatlar**
rights	**huquqlar**
seismic survey	**seysmolozhi tädqiqat**
supply *noun*	**täjhizat**
well	**quyu**
well site	**quyu qazıma mä'däni**

31. TIME AND DATES

century	**yüzillik**
decade	**onillik**
year	**il**
month	**ay**
fortnight	**iki häftä**
week	**häftä**
day	**gün**
hour	**saat**
minute	**däqiqä**
second	**saniyä**

dawn	**shäfäq**
sunrise	**gündoghan**
morning	**sähär**
daytime	**gündüz**
noon	**günorta**
afternoon	**günortadan sonra**
evening	**akhsham**
sunset	**qurub; günbatan**
night	**gejä**
midnight	**gejä yarısı**

four days before	**dörd gün ävväl**
three days before	**üch gün ävväl**
the day before yesterday	**sıragha gün**
yesterday	**dünän**
today	**bugün**
tomorrow	**sabah**
the day after tomorrow	**birisi gün**
three days from now	**üch gün sonra**
four days from now	**dörd gün sonra**

the year before last	kechän ildän bir il qabagh
last year	kechän il
this year	bu il
next year	növbäti il
the year after next	növbäti ildän bir il sonra
last week	kechän häftä
this week	bu häftä
next week	gälän häftä
this morning	bu sähär
now	indi
tonight	bu akhsham
yesterday morning	dünän sähär
yesterday afternoon	dünän gündüz
yesterday night	dünän gejä
tomorrow morning	sabah sähär
tomorrow afternoon	sabah gündüz
tomorrow night	sabah gejä (akhsham)
in the morning	sahar vakhtı
in the afternoon	gündüz vakhtı
in the evening	akhsham vakhtı
past	kechmish
present	mövjud
future	gäläjäk
What date is it today?	Bu gün hansı gündür?
What time is it?	Saat nechädir?
It is . . . o'clock.	Saat . . . dir.

SEASONS

summer	yay
autumn	payız
winter	qısh
spring	yaz

DAYS OF THE WEEK

Monday	**bazar ertäsi**
Tuesday	**chärshänbä akhshamı**
Wednesday	**chärshänbä**
Thursday	**jümä akhshamı**
Friday	**jümä**
Saturday	**shänbä**
Sunday	**bazar**

MONTHS

January	**yanvar**
February	**fevral**
March	**mart**
April	**aprel**
May	**may**
June	**iyun**
July	**iyul**
August	**avqust**
September	**sentyabr**
October	**oktyabr**
November	**noyabr**
December	**dekabr**

32. NUMBERS AND AMOUNTS

0	**sıfr**
1	**bir**
2	**iki**
3	**üch**
4	**dörd**
5	**besh**
6	**altı**
7	**yeddi**
8	**säkkiz**
9	**doqquz**
10	**on**
11	**on bir**
12	**on iki**
13	**on üch**
14	**on dörd**
15	**on besh**
16	**on altı**
17	**on yeddi**
18	**on säkkiz**
19	**on doqquz**
20	**iyirmi**
22	**iyirmi iki**
30	**otuz**
32	**otuz iki**
40	**qırkh**
42	**qırkh iki**
50	**älli**
52	**älli iki**
60	**altmısh**
62	**altmısh iki**
70	**yetmish**
72	**yetmish iki**
80	**säksän**
82	**säksän iki**

90	**dokhsan**
92	**dokhsan iki**
100	**yüz**
102	**yüz iki**
112	**yüz on iki**
200	**iki yüz**
300	**üch yüz**
400	**dörd yüz**
500	**besh yüz**
600	**altı yüz**
700	**yeddi yüz**
800	**säkkiz yüz**
900	**doqquz yüz**
1,000	**min**
10,000	**on min**
50,000	**älli min**
100,000	**yüz min**
1,000,000	**bir milyon**
first	**birinji**
second	**ikinji**
third	**üchünjü**
fourth	**dördünjü**
tenth	**onunju**
fifteenth	**onbeshinji**
twentieth	**iyirminji**
once	**bir däfä**
twice	**iki däfä**
three times	**üch däfä**
one-half	**yarısı**
one-quarter	**dörddäbir**
three-quarters	**dördäüch**
one-third	**üchdäbir**
two-thirds	**üchdäiki**

WEIGHTS & MEASURES

kilometer	**kilometr**
meter	**metr**
mile	**mil**
foot	**fut**
yard	**yard**
gallon	**qalon**
liter	**litr**
kilogram	**kiloqram**
gram	**qram**
pound	**funt**
ounce	**untsiya**

33. OPPOSITES

beginning—end	**ävväli—sonu**
clean—dirty	**tämiz—chirkin**
comfortable—uncomfortable	**rahat—narahat**
fertile—barren *land*	**bähräli—barsız**
happy—unhappy	**khoshbäkht—qämli**
life—death —	**häyat—ölüm**
friend—enemy	**dost—düshmän**
modern—traditional	**müasir—änänävi**
modern—ancient	**müasir—qädim**
open—shut	**achıq—baghlı**
wide—narrow	**genish—dar**
high—low	**yüksäk/uca—ashaghı/alchaq**
peace—violence/war	**sülh—zorakılıq/müharibä**
polite—rude	**näzakätli—kobud**
silence—noise	**sükut—säs-küy**
cheap—expensive	**ujuz—baha**
hot/warm—cold/cool	**isti/ilıq—soyuq/särin**
health—disease	**saghlamlıq—khästälik**
well—sick	**saghlam—khästä**
night—day	**gejä—gündüz**
top—bottom	**zirvä—dib**
backwards—forwards	**geriyä—iräliyä**
back—front	**arkha—qabagh**
dead—alive	**ölü—diri/sagh**
near—far	**yakhın—uzaq**
left—right	**sol—sagh**
in—out	**ichäriyä—kharijä**
up—down	**yukharı—ashaghı**
yes—no	**hä/bäli—yokh/kheyr**
here—there	**burada—orada**
soft—hard	**yumshaq—bärk**
easy—difficult	**yüngül—chätin**
quick—slow	**tez—yavash**

big—small	**böyük—balaja**
old—young	**goja—javan**
tall—short	**uja—alchaq**
strong—weak	**güjlü—zäif**
success—failure	**ughur—mäghlubiyyät**
new—old	**täzä—köhnä**
question—answer	**sual—javab**
safety—danger	**tählükäsizlik—tählükä**
good—bad	**yakhshı—pis**
true—false	**häqiqi—yalan**
light—heavy	**yüngül—aghır**
light—darkness	**ushıq—qaranlıq**
well—badly	**yakhshı—pis**
truth—lie	**häqiqät—uydurma**

The best – and most accessible – introduction to Azerbaijan, its people, cultures and languages currently available is *The Azerbaijanis: A Handbook*, edited by Nicholas Awde (Curzon Press, London). The only history available is *Azerbaijan: A Quest for Identity*, by Charles van der Leeuw, who has also written a brief history of the eceonomic development of the area, *Oil and Gas in the Caucasus & Caspian: A History* (both Curzon Press, London).

~

AZERBAIJAN

Maps by Emanuela Losi